Study Guide
to
CHINA

Adapting the Past
Confronting the Future

THOMAS BUOYE

CENTER FOR CHINESE STUDIES
THE UNIVERSITY OF MICHIGAN
ANN ARBOR

Published by Center for Chinese Studies
The University of Michigan
Ann Arbor, Michigan 48104-1608

First Edition 2003

Printed and made in the United States of America

The paper used in this publication meets the minimum
requirements of the American National Standard for Information
Sciences—Permanence of Paper for Publications and Documents
in Libraries and Archives ANSI/NISO/Z39.48—1992.

ISBN 0-89264-157-6

Contents

Preface

China: Adapting the Past, Confronting the Future introduces contemporary China through an array of materials that includes historical documents, scholarly articles, ethnographic studies, Chinese literature, and Western media reports. The result is a comprehensive book that reflects the complexity and diversity of China today. This *Study Guide* is an important adjunct to the textbook. It helps students to integrate and assimilate the diverse materials and opinions presented there. Inevitably, not every point of view can be represented and the editors have suggested further readings to supplement the materials presented. The *Study Guide* also provides recommendations for relevant films and documentaries as well as a wide-ranging list of Internet sites that point the student toward additional resources.

Students will find the *Study Guide* helpful as they seek to consolidate their understanding of the many complex issues they will encounter. Like the editors' introductions in *China: Adapting the Past, Confronting the Future*, which provide context and perspective for the readings, the *Study Guide* proposes strategies for assimilating and retaining the essential points. Neither the editors' introductions nor the *Study Guide* can substitute for careful study of the readings themselves, however.

The organization of the *Study Guide* follows that of *China: Adapting the Past, Confronting the Future* the *Study Guide*, with six major parts—History and Geography, Politics, Economy, Society, Culture, and Future Trends. Each unit contains a list of the readings and a set of *Learning Objectives*. An *Overview* summarizes the readings and highlights the major themes. A list of pertinent *Web Links* and *Documentary and Feature Film* suggestions is also provided, and each unit contains a glossary of *Key Concepts* that clarifies unfamiliar terms. Finally, *Review Questions* are provided to help students test their grasp of the factual content of the readings as well as the broader themes of the unit. The *Study Guide* presents a list of *Essay / Discussion Questions* that requires students to synthesize what they have learned and demonstrate comprehension of its larger significance. The final two sections, *Online Resources* and *Video and Film*, provide a comprehensive list of Internet resources related to China and suggestions for complementary multi-part video series and films. This section will undoubtedly be of interest to students and instructors alike.

***

Many different systems have been used for rendering Chinese words and names in the Roman alphabet. The system currently used in most English-language scholarship and journalism is pinyin, the system officially endorsed by the People's Republic of China. This system used in this *Study Guide*, in the editors' Introductions in *China: Adapting the Past, Confronting the Future*, and in many of the readings. However, much literature on China employs the older Wade-Giles system, still used by some scholars and in some readings in the textbook. While students of China quickly learn that "Mao Zedong" (pinyin) is the same as "Mao Tse-tung," (Wade-Giles) the different forms can be confusing. The appendix to this *Study Guide* contains both a pinyin pronunciation guide and a complete pinyin/Wade-Giles conversion chart. Finally, the spellings of certain names, like "Confucius" and "Peking" belong to neither system but are commonly used in English.

Geography and History

This section introduces the geographic and historical factors that provide keys to understanding contemporary China. Highlighting the ethnic and environmental diversity and major developments in Chinese history from earliest times to the twentieth century, this section focuses on the influence of the past on the people of China as they face the challenges of the modern world.

Readings

1. "China's Environmental History in World Perspective," by J. R. McNeil
2. "The Uniting of China," by Dru Gladney
3. "Confucius," by John E. Will, Jr.
4. "History and China's Revolution," by John King Fairbank
5. "A Proclamation Against the Bandits of Guangdong and Guangxi, 1854," by Zeng Guofan
6. "The Boxer Uprising," by Paul A. Cohen
7. "The Chinese Enlightenment," by Vera Schwarcz
8. "Sun Yat-sen Opens the Whampoa Academy, 1924," by Sun Yat-sen
9. "Report on an Investigation of the Peasant Movement in Hunan," by Mao Zedong
10. "Collapse of Public Morale on the Eve of Communist Takeover," by A. Doak Barnett
11. "The Exclusion Act May 6, 1882"
12. "Chinese Anti-Foreignism, 1892"

Learning Objectives

To become acquainted with:
- the geographic and cultural diversity of China
- a general outline of Chinese history
- Confucius and the principal tenets of his thought

1

- the historical antecedents of China's struggle to modernize
- the legacy of Sino-American relations

Overview

The articles by J. R. McNeil and Dru Gladney highlight China's rich geographic and ethnic diversity. China has often been portrayed erroneously as unchanging and homogeneous, but nothing could be further from the truth. As McNeil's article illustrates, the country in fact spans a broad range of climatic zones and possesses a rich bounty of varied natural resources. Centuries of human labor have in many areas transformed the landscape. A brief analysis of China's ecological history explodes the myth that because Asian philosophies stress harmony between man and nature, they have restrained human alteration of the natural environment. In fact, by the eighteenth century, the destruction of China's forests and manipulation of its surface water gave rise to ecological stresses on a par with, if not greater than, that of other countries in the world. Rapid industrial expansion, urban sprawl, and an increased use of chemical fertilizers over the past two decades has once again raised the specter of environmental crisis.

Dru Gladney's article delineates China's linguistic and ethnic diversity. The present government officially recognizes fifty-six minority nationalities. Although the Han nationality represents roughly 90 percent of the total population, it is important to note that the remaining 10 percent is equal to about 130 million people. Many of the ethnic nationalities live in the sparsely inhabited western half of country or at strategic points along China's borders to the north and south. China has a long history as a multiethnic country, and as recently as the Qing dynasty (1644–1911) China's rulers were Manchu, a minority people from the north. As Gladney notes, ethnic unity has been an important goal for revolutionary movements in the twentieth century for idealistic as well as strategic reasons. Both the Guomindang (GMD) and the Chinese Communist Party (CCP) actively sought to develop ethnic policies that would unify the nation. The results have not completely succeeded and, given the complicated history of China's relationship to its neighbors and the break-up of the Soviet Union, ethnic separatism remains a major concern for China's leaders.

Chinese civilization has survived for over 4,000 years, and while no summary can adequately do justice to its complexity and splendor, Thomas Buoye's introductory essay provides a succinct outline of the Chinese past. The essay begins by introducing key developments in early Chinese history, including the origins of Confucian thought, and the third century B.C. founding of the Qin dynasty, which established a centralized bureaucratic state that remained the hallmark of traditional polity for all subsequent dynasties. The life and thought of Confucius, China's premier moral philosopher, are introduced in John Wills' article. Confucian thought has undergone centuries of reinterpretation but its basic principles still exert a strong influence in China and throughout East Asia. Important developments in later dynasties are briefly examined before Buoye turns to the Qing dynasty (1644–1911) and the Republican era (1911–1949). The essay notes that China faced enormous social, economic, and political challenges prior to the advent of militant commercial powers from the West and the disastrous Opium War (1839–1841). Government officials, Chinese intellectuals, and the common people all faced difficult choices as they struggled to restructure their government, their economy, and their personal lives in response to challenges posed by both domestic and outside forces. Some chose restoration of traditional values, others chose reform, borrowing knowledge and institutions from the West but maintaining faith in Chinese ethical and cultural values. Ultimately, many chose revolution, seeking fundamental change in Chinese political and social institutions. As the essay and readings demonstrate, the struggle was psychologically and physically grueling, not to mention extremely bloody.

John Fairbank's article lays out the broad dimensions of the dilemma that China faced in the nineteenth century, beset by foreign invasion and burdened by traditional institutions badly in need of reform. Still, the Qing dynasty managed to survive massive internal upheavals and the ongoing threat of foreign intervention in large part thanks to loyal Han Chinese officials like Zeng Guofan, author of the proclamation that successfully rallied elite support to defend the Manchu dynasty against the Taipings. It was not until the last decade of the Qing dynasty that Han Chinese openly began to decry the Qing on ethnic grounds. After surviving the Taiping Rebellion, the Qing embarked on a conservative program of reform known as the Self-strengthening Movement. This effort was ultimately deemed a failure after China's shocking defeat in the Sino-Japanese War (1894–1895). Many scholars believe the Qing dynasty reached its nadir after the Boxer Uprising described by Paul Cohen's article. A final decade of sweeping reform followed in the wake of the Boxer Uprising, but it was too late to save the Qing.

The establishment of a republican government after the overthrow of the Qing dynasty was not the panacea many Chinese revolutionaries had sought. The rise of warlordism and the ongoing imperialist threat motivated many Chinese intellectuals to seek more thoroughgoing and more radical reforms. Vera Schwarcz's discussion of the May Fourth Movement and the new generation of young radicals succinctly illustrates the new turn the Chinese struggle to modernize took after 1919. Intellectuals had always played an important role in Chinese politics, but in the post-May Fourth era that role was redefined to include revolutionary action. In addition to creating new political parties, Sun Yat-sen, the first modern Chinese revolutionary, had learned after years of bitter experience that military power was essential. Sun, with support from the Soviet Union, established the Whampoa Military Academy to train his officers. His speech (reading 8), emphasizes the need to instill patriotic and revolutionary values in the military. Mao Zedong, who dominated the Chinese Communist Party after 1935, understood the importance of military force, but he also understood the plight of the overwhelming majority of the Chinese population, the peasantry. Mao's report on the peasant movement in Hunan reveals his early commitment to a peasant-based strategy of revolution.

By 1927, the Guomindang under the leadership of Chiang Kai-shek managed to establish a national government in Nanjing, and throughout the 1930s a major goal of Chiang's was elimination of the Communists. The CCP had subsequently gone underground in the cities or had taken refuge in the rural bases like Mao's Jiangxi Soviet. The struggle between the GMD and CCP was fought against the background of Japanese imperialism that turned into full-scale invasion and occupation from 1937 to 1945. During this period the fortunes of the CCP rose while the image of the GMD became tarnished. As A. Doak Barnett's reportage during the period of civil war indicates, the GMD defeat was partly of their own making. Although many Chinese were only dimly aware of the goals of the Communists, the war-weary country was ready for a new government in 1949. The final two readings are primary sources that reveal the depth of misunderstanding between China and the U.S., misunderstanding that has roots as far back as the nineteenth century.

Web Links

There are a number of excellent websites for Chinese geography and history:
WWW-VL: History: China (http://www.ukans.edu/history/VL/east_asia/china.html)
is an essential starting point for online resources on geography and history.

An excellent collection of detailed, thematic, and historical maps of China can be found online at the Perry-Castañeda Library Map Collection (http://www.lib.utexas.edu/maps/china.html).

A report by the International Institute for Applied Systems Analysis entitled "Can China Feed Itself?" as well as datasets, maps, graphs, and links can be found at http://www.iiasa.ac.at/Research/LUC/ChinaFood/index_m.htm.

A variety of good websites on Chinese history include text, primary sources, and images. Paul Halsall's Internet East Asian History Sourcebook (http://www.fordham.edu/halsall/eastasia/eastasiasbook.html) is among the better sites. For Confucian thought and early Chinese philosophy, Chad Hansen's Chinese Philosophy Pages (http://www.hku.hk/philodep/ch/) is an excellent starting point. Additional web resources are discussed in the **Online Resources** section at the end of the book.

Documentary and Feature Film Suggestions

Eating, from the series *The Chinese,* introduces the geographic diversity and the regional specialties of Chinese cuisine though an examination of eating. The exotic dishes of southern China are juxtaposed with the simple fare of rural families in the north. An updated version of this segment would need to address the proliferation of American fast food restaurants in Chinese cities. An excellent documentary video for the Republican period (1912–1949) is *China in Revolution.* The video consists of two one-hour segments and combines historical footage and personal interviews with participants. The result is a compelling and sometimes poignant film that puts a human face on the political upheavals of the Republican period.

Chinese feature films are often too long to screen during normal class times; still, they make excellent teaching resources. Early Chinese history is vividly depicted in *The Emperor and the Assassin*, a lush historical drama about the rise to power of the first Chinese emperor. *The Opium War* depicts events leading up to the clash between China and Great Britain in the nineteenth century. Released to coincide with the return of Hong Kong to Chinese control, this film provides a Chinese perspective on the war. Many other excellent movies deal with historical events in the nineteenth and twentieth centuries. One film that illustrates the plight of women in traditional China is *Ju Dou*, an erotic thriller dramatizing the oppressiveness of traditional society.

Key Concepts

"*Mandate of Heaven.*" The concept of the Mandate of Heaven can be traced to the founding of the Zhou dynasty (1122–256 B.C.). The rulers of the Zhou claimed that Heaven, conceived as a moral force that governed the universe, had legitimated their overthrow of the wicked ruler of their predecessors, the Shang dynasty (1766–1122 B.C.) and the establishment of a new dynasty. Thus, the "virtue" of an emperor became the ethical sanction for maintaining his rule. Confucius and his followers incorporated this idea into their beliefs. Some later Confucians even argued that the immoral conduct of an emperor effectively removed his mandate and justified rebellion. During the later Han dynasty (202 B.C.–6 A.D.) Confucian scholars had come to believe that natural phenomenon, such as earthquakes or super novas, could be interpreted as Heaven's displeasure with a ruler.

"*Three Sage Kings.*" According to legend, Yao, Shun, and Yu were the first three rulers of China. Although no historical evidence of them exists and surviving accounts of their skills and virtues make them iconic rather than complex human figures, scholars of Confucius' time considered them to be historical rulers, and Confucius, and his followers in particular, held them up as exemplars of wiser rule.

Legalism. The doctrine of Legalism, which supplied the ideological and political foundation for China's first dynasty, the Qin (221–206 B.C.), stressed the rational organization of society and resources to strengthen the state. Legalists argued that human nature was evil and that elaborate laws backed up by severe punishments were the key to expanding state power and keeping people submissive and disciplined.

Literati. Western sinologists often use the term "literati" to refer to the highly educated elites who historically were the primary source of government officials in China. The term literati is appropriate since after the Tang dynasty (619–908 A.D.) most officials achieved office through the civil service examination system, which tested their knowledge of the classics of ancient literature, particularly those of Confucius and his followers. Since only the wealthy could reasonably afford the education needed to succeed in the examinations, and since most wealth was derived from agriculture, some modern scholars also use the term "gentry" to refer to this group. Other terms include "scholar-gentry," which captures both sources of their influence, and "scholar-officials."

Civil Service Examination System. The civil service examination system had its origins in the Han dynasty but did not become the most important route to government office until the Song dynasty (960–1279 A.D.). The content of the examinations was based primarily on the Confucian classics. Mastery of the knowledge needed to pass the examinations required rigorous study that usually began in early childhood. The examinations normally took place triennially and at three levels: local, provincial, and national. Only those who passed the national-level examinations were guaranteed a position in government, but obtaining a degree at any level marked an individual as a member of the elite and man of influence. The eventual imposition of quotas on the number of degrees granted meant that many otherwise talented individuals were frustrated in their goal of obtaining office. The civil service examination system lasted until 1905 when it was abolished during the late Qing reforms (1901–1911).

"Imperialism" and *"Feudalism."* As used by John Fairbank in reading 4, imperialism broadly refers to the eighteenth- through twentieth-century burden of special privileges for foreign powers in China, including economic and financial dominance, the missionary presence, and military interventions. Feudalism broadly refers to the traditional domestic political, social, and cultural institutions that were considered an obstacle to modern development, including autocratic rule, the political and cultural supremacy of the literati class, the patriarchal family system, and Confucian teachings.

Treaty Port System. One condition of the Treaty of Nanjing, which ended the Opium War in 1842, was that China would open a total of five ports to trade and allow foreigners to live and work in these ports. Shanghai, one of the original five ports, quickly became the most important center of foreign trade and home to the largest foreign community in China. The number of treaty ports expanded from five in 1842 to about fifty by 1911. The term "treaty port system" refers to the lifestyles and institutions of the foreign communities, which were exempt from Chinese law. In addition to their economic activities, foreigners built homes, churches, schools, and libraries. Ironically, these symbols of foreign domination were often safe havens for Chinese dissidents and revolutionaries who sought to overthrow the Qing dynasty and restore national pride.

Self-strengthening Movement. After the suppression of the Taiping Rebellion in 1864, Chinese sought to reform their traditional institutions while simultaneously importing technology from West. This was undertaken under the banner of self-strengthening. The "*ti-yong* formula," named for the Chinese characters *ti* (essence or substance) and *yong* (use or means), can be summarized as "Chinese learning as the substance, Western learning as the means." A variety of powerful provincial officials individually engaged in this type of reform. The failure of their efforts was apparent in 1895 when Japan, which had undergone more extensive reforms during the same period, defeated China in Sino-Japanese War.

Scramble for Concessions (1898). In the wake of China's defeat in the Sino-Japanese War, Japan demanded exclusive control over Chinese territory in Manchuria. After Germany, France, and Russia intervened, Japan dropped this demand. Shortly thereafter, however, Russia demanded exclusive control over Chinese territory in the same area, touching off a spate of similar demands from the other major powers. One by one, the European powers and Japan obtained leaseholds over Chinese territories that included mining and railway rights, and permission to station troops and naval forces. Unlike the treaty ports these new leaseholds directly and extensively intruded on local communities. This intrusion often triggered violent backlashes, which, in turn, embroiled the Qing government in disputes with the foreign powers. In reaction to these developments, the United States, which had not taken part in the Scramble for Concessions, proposed the Open Door Policy that called for respecting China's sovereignty and territorial integrity.

May Fourth Movement. On May 4, 1919, Chinese students in Beijing held major demonstrations to protest the government's acceptance of provisions in the Versailles Treaty granting Germany's former concessions in Shandong Province to Japan. The movement spread to other major Chinese cities and drew support from merchants, workers, and intellectuals. For the first time in Chinese history people of all classes across the country gave expression to a new sense of nationalism. What became known as the May Fourth Movement grew out of those 1919 demonstrations. The movement was marked by a vociferous rejection of traditional culture and greater political activism by intellectuals. The combination of political and cultural goals became evident in the linguistic and literary reforms promoted to make literature more accessible and relevant to all Chinese people.

Republican Period (1912–1949). After the Qing dynasty's overthrow in the Revolution of 1911, the first republican government was formed. Throughout this period Chinese politicians struggled to unify their country and establish a modern state. In fact, large parts of China remained outside central government control during this period.

Warlord Era (1916–1927). After the death of China's President Yuan Shikai (1859–1916), who had prepared to install himself as an emperor prior to his demise, military governors of several provinces consolidated control of their own regions. These "warlords" then fought among themselves for territorial dominance until 1927 when China was unified under the Guomindang or Nationalist Party. In reality, Guomindang control was tenuous at best, and several major warlords retained local control while pledging allegiance to the new government.

Marriage Law of 1950. One of the first social reforms of the new Communist regime, the Marriage Law of 1950 outlawed traditional arranged marriages. The law enhanced women's rights and also undermined the power of male clan leaders and heads of families.

Review Questions

1. How did China's ecological diversity contribute to the stability and unity of the Chinese empire? What have been the two greatest environmental changes in the last three thousand years? What new challenges has China faced during the last two decades of rapid economic growth?

2. Historically China has always been a multi-ethnic society, though what we refer to today as the Han-Chinese nationality has always been dominant. According to Gladney, how was the notion of "Han ren" reinterpreted in the twentieth century? What were the circumstances under which this reinterpretation took place? How has the current regime's nationality policy evolved since 1949?

3. China's long history has been viewed as a series of successive dynasties that face inevitable decline and replacement by a new dynasty. This cyclical model asserts little fundamental change in political, economic, or social institutions over time. How useful is it for understanding China's past? According to Buoye, how did the decline of the Qing differ significantly from that of previous dynasties?

4. Despite the twin burdens of "imperialism" and "feudalism" described by Fairbank, the Qing dynasty survived until 1911. The Taiping Rebellion was perhaps the greatest internal threat of the nineteenth century. On what grounds did Zeng Guofan appeal to Chinese elites to defend the Qing?

5. Why does Buoye claim that the Boxer Uprising manifests all the social and political dilemmas of the Qing dynasty? To what extent can the origins of the uprising be attributed to the "feudalism" or "imperialism" described by Fairbank?

6. The May Fourth Movement marked an important turning point in the Chinese struggle to modernize. According to Schwarcz, how did May Fourth intellectuals seek to reform Chinese culture in their effort launch China on the genuine path to modernity? What significance did the establishment of the Whampoa Military Academy have in China's modernization?

7. According to Mao Zedong "... a revolution is not a dinner party, or writing an essay, or painting a picture, or doing embroidery; it cannot be so refined, so leisurely and gentle, so temperate, kind, courteous, restrained and magnanimous." What did Mao mean by this statement and to whom were his remarks addressed? In the struggle between the GMD and CCP what internal and external factors contributed to their failure and success?

8. How have Sino-American relations changed over the past century? How have mutual misconceptions plagued this relationship? What are some of the issues that continue to shape Sino-American relations?

Politics

This section examines political developments in China since the establishment of the People's Republic of China in 1949. From 1949 until his death in 1976, Mao Zedong dominated the political landscape. But as the Chinese Communist Party pursued the daunting goals of national unification, social transformation, and modernization, the leadership was often embroiled in serious political and personal conflicts. Since Mao's death, dramatic changes have occurred, but as these readings demonstrate, despite more than a quarter century of economic growth and relative political stability, the current Chinese leadership continues to face serious political challenges.

Readings

13. "The Beijing Upheaval of 1989," by Andrew Walder
14. "China since Tiananmen Square," by Stanley Rosen
15. "Human Rights in China," by Andrew Nathan
16. "Chinese Nationalistic Writing in the 1990s," by Suisheng Zhao
17. "A Quiet Roar," by Eric Eckholm
18. "China's Emerging Business Class: Democracy's Harbinger?"
    by Margaret M. Pearson
19. "Village Elections: Democracy from the Bottom Up?" by Tyrene White
20. "The Virus of Corruption," by James Miles

Learning Objectives

To become acquainted with:
- the structure of political organization in China since 1949
- the challenges posed to Communist ideology in the era of economic reforms
- the changing nature of political participation in contemporary China
- the sources of political dissent and protest

11

- the new Chinese nationalism in the post-Mao era
- the issues that shape Sino-American relations

Overview

Professor Dickson's introductory essay describes the three immediate and practical goals of Mao Zedong and the Chinese Communist Party (CCP) in 1949: national unification, transformation of traditional Chinese institutions, and modernization of the economy. After decades of internal division and foreign invasion, the Chinese people, regardless of political orientation, all desired national unification, and the CCP enjoyed a good measure of popular support in 1949. The CCP had some early successes in transforming society, most notably through land reform, which provided land to the largest sector of China's population, the poor peasants. Similarly, the Marriage Law of 1950 granted women new rights and outlawed the traditional custom of arranged marriages.

Modernization of the economy was more difficult. Using Soviet-style economic planning, China experienced impressive industrial growth during its first five-year plan (1952–1957), but China's leaders were divided over the political and social implications of Soviet-style economic development. As Professor Dickson's essay explains, Mao Zedong played a critical leadership role as policy shifted between economic development and ideological priorities. When Mao's grand scheme to pursue both economic development and ideological transformation simultaneously, the ill-conceived and poorly executed "Great Leap Forward" (1958–1959) ended in tragic failure, the stage was set for the political leadership struggles that culminated in Mao's launching of the Cultural Revolution in 1966. The political repercussions of the Cultural Revolution lasted until Mao's death in 1976. Mao's belief that Chinese leaders' "loss of revolutionary fervor" and their growing hostility toward his policies and his personal style of leadership within the CCP were the root causes of the Cultural Revolution. But as the movement spread and took on a life of its own, it embroiled the nation in a decade of sometimes violent political struggle. The Cultural Revolution left a deep scar on Chinese society, particularly among the generation of youthful Red Guards who answered Mao's call to rebel against the party, and it shattered faith in ideological solutions to social and economic development. Despite the disasters of the Cultural Revolution, Mao's personal prestige remained intact. It was only after Mao died that Deng Xiaoping and his supporters could begin to implement the economic reforms that have transformed China.

Despite the shift in economic policy, the CCP inherited several problems from the Maoist era that it is has yet to completely remedy. For example, the party leadership made decisions collectively immediately after Mao's death, but then anointed Deng Xiaoping paramount leader, which he remained until his death in 1997. Similarly, the CCP has also tried to restore power to formal government institutions such as the National People's Congress (NPC), which during the Maoist era had been a rubber-stamp parliament. Over the past two decades the NPC has played a more active, though still subordinate, role, passing laws that it drafted and debated and overseeing the operation of the government. Another challenge has been reviving the CCP itself. After Mao, the party suffered from low morale and a shortage of technically skilled members. Under Deng, the party gradually eased older, often less educated, members into retirement and recruited new members from a broader spectrum of society. As a consequence, the average age of party members has declined while their average level of education has increased. In 2001 the CCP even lifted its ban on recruiting from the emerging class of private entrepreneurs, though, as Margaret Pearson's article explains, their inclusion has yet to produce major political changes.

Under Deng Xiaoping's leadership, the overwhelming majority of the Chinese people saw their standard of living rise. China became more open to the rest of the world and party control over society was substantially relaxed. Nevertheless, in the decades since Mao's death, the CCP has jealously guarded its monopoly on political power and ruthlessly suppressed any threats to that power. From 1978–1979, the CCP tolerated "The Democracy Wall Movement," during which citizens criticized the excesses of the Maoist era. But once calls for greater democracy and radical political reform arose from this arena of criticism, the CCP suppressed the movement. Similarly, student demonstrations in 1986–1987 were initially tolerated but eventually suppressed. By 1989, political corruption and double-digit inflation fueled renewed demands for political change and led to the Tiananmen crisis. For two months in the late spring, Beijing became the scene of a student-led political demonstration that quickly gained popular support and sparked similar protests in other Chinese cities. As Andrew Walder's article notes, in light of broad access to modern communications and foreign news reports, which related the collapse of communist regimes in Eastern Europe, the CCP at first appeared divided in its response.

Eventually, however, the army was summoned to suppress the demonstrations with lethal force, and although the death toll from the crackdown remains in dispute, there were likely hundreds killed.

In the aftermath of the Tiananmen crisis, China's future seemed uncertain. Domestically, popular resentment and outrage toward the CCP and the army simmered beneath the surface, while foreign governments condemned the brutality and foreign investors reevaluated their positions. The CCP steadfastly and publicly rejected domestic and foreign condemnation of its brutality, but the leadership privately acknowledged that something needed to be done to revive the economy and restore popular support for the party and the government. The result over the past decade has been an interesting balancing act. On the one hand, the CCP has expanded the program of economic reform begun under Deng to the point where China has now been accepted for membership in the World Trade Organization (WTO). Politically, as Tyrene White's article points out, the CCP has made tentative but significant steps toward democratic reform at the grass roots level. On the other hand, the crackdown on the Falun Gong movement served as a reminder that the CCP will not tolerate any threat, real or imagined, to its authority. Eschewing appeals to ideology, the CCP has encouraged a new Chinese nationalism described in the article by Suisheng Zhao. Stanley Rosen's article notes that this nationalism resonates powerfully with today's Chinese students, whose interests and political orientations have changed significantly since 1989.

Rising Chinese nationalism and ongoing disagreements over human rights will undoubtedly complicate future Sino-American relations. As Andrew Nathan, an eloquent critic of China's human rights policy, explains in his article, by any reasonable standard, human rights remain a problem in China. Here the U.S. should play a leadership role, but a growing number of Chinese view any U.S. efforts to improve human rights as hypocritical interference in China's internal affairs. Human rights and the "virus of corruption" that James Miles describes are problems that appear to have no simple or immediate solutions. As the materials in this section demonstrate, China has made enormous progress economically and, to a lesser extent, politically, since the death of Mao, but much remains to be done.

Web Links

For tracking current events, *Inside China Today* at (http://www.einnews.com/china/) provides breaking news on China and more than two hundred other countries.

Human Rights in China (http://iso.hrichina.org/iso/) is a website that monitors conditions in China and provides downloadable reports.

For international affairs, the National Committee on U.S.-China Relations website (http://www.ncuscr.org/index.htm) supplies current news on Sino-American relations.

For students interested in research on major events in the history of Sino-American relations, reports and primary sources, including declassified government intelligence reports, can be found at the *Archive Resources on U.S.-China Relations* (http://www.gwu.edu/~nsarchiv/NSAEBB/NSAEBB41/).

For more information about relations between China and Taiwan, the site, *Taiwan Security Research* (http://taiwansecurity.org/TSR-PRC.htm) is a particularly useful site.

Many sites focus on the Tiananmen crisis of 1989: *The Gate of Heavenly Peace* (http://www.tsquare.tv/) is maintained by the Long Bow Group, makers of several award winning documentaries including *The Gate of Heavenly Peace*. The site includes video clips, transcripts of interviews, additional readings and web links, and historical background on the event. (See **Online Resources** for additional sites related to politics.)

Documentary and Feature Film Suggestions

China: The Mao Years is a gripping documentary covering the Maoist era (1949–1976). This film effectively combines historical footage and individual interviews with participants, including former Red Guards and CCP officials. Coverage of the Cultural Revolution is particularly vivid and moving. The Long Bow Group's documentary on the Tiananmen crisis, *The Gate of Heavenly Peace* tells the story of the bloody suppression of the 1989 demonstrations. It also intersperses live footage and interviews from 1989, with subsequent interviews of participants done in the 1990s. Since the film focuses on student demonstrations, many instructors find it particularly effective for classroom use. *Believing* from the series *The Chinese* examines traditional Chinese ideology and the eclipse of communist principles during the early years of economic reform. Interestingly, many of the worst fears expressed by CCP officials regarding the abandonment of communist ideals and a growing consumer mentality in 1980s have now been realized.

Several recent feature films address the politics of the Maoist era. *The Blue Kite* examines impacts of the shifting political policies on the life of a family in Beijing. *To Live* takes a similar approach, but begins in the pre-1949 era. Both films present a very personal perspective on politics. Similarly, they both demonstrate the resiliency of the family as an institution despite traumatic political upheavals. The betrayal of Mao's Red Guards in the Cultural Revolution is tragically portrayed in *Xiu Xiu, The Sent Down Girl.*

Key Concepts

National People's Congress is the China's supreme lawmaking body. In the post-Mao era it has gone from a rubber-stamp institution to a potential challenger to the CCP's monopoly on power. To date it has not directly challenged the party, but members now sponsor their own bills; debate is active and dissent is evident.

Hundred Flowers Movement (1957). Mao invited intellectuals and experts who were not party members to criticize CCP's performance. Assuming the CCP had been successful and generated support for the regime, Mao was unexpectedly put on the defensive when strong and fundamental criticisms of the new political system appeared. In a harsh backlash Mao labeled the critics "rightists" and counterrevolutionaries. During the subsequent "Anti-Rightist Campaign" many of these critics were persecuted and sentenced to "reform through labor." Those surviving their reform experience carried the lifelong stigma of the rightist label.

Great Leap Forward (1958–1959). Dissatisfied with the lack of progress in the socialist transformation of Chinese society, in 1958 Mao Zedong launched an overly ambitious and ultimately disastrous mass campaign known as the Great Leap Forward. The Great Leap Forward stressed mass mobilization, political education, and self-reliance; it was designed to increase agricultural and industrial productivity while simultaneously reorganizing society. Poor planning, the withdrawal of aid from the Soviet Union, and bad weather compounded the disaster and lead to severe famine in some regions.

"Three Bad Years" (1960–1962). The failure of the Great Leap had both immediate and long-term consequences. The devastating impact of the agricultural failures was felt most severely during the "Three Bad Years," when an estimated 30 million people starved to death.

Cultural Revolution. The Cultural Revolution was a major political and social upheaval that affected all aspects of life in China for nearly a decade. Mao Zedong launched the Cultural Revolution in 1966 as a means to realize his personal vision of socialist modernization. What began as a debate in literary circles soon evolved into a criticism of all remnants of Chinese tradition. It became a mass movement led by young Red Guards who took the writings and words of Mao as their guide to action. Individuals, especially intellectuals, were physically attacked and sent to the countryside to learn from the peasants. Schools closed and the economy came to a standstill. Eventually, the army had to be called in to restore order when struggles between competing factions turned violent. The movement was also a power struggle at the highest levels of the party, during which Mao ruthlessly eliminated his political opponents.

Red Guards. Chinese students who formed paramilitary groups known as Red Guards were a critical element of support for Mao Zedong during the early stages of the Cultural Revolution. Mao urges students to challenge authority and attack elements in the CCP who were pursuing, according to Mao, capitalist policies. Red Guard units proliferated across China in answer to Mao's call. They were fanatically devoted to Mao and often resorted to violence against Mao's political enemies. As the Cultural Revolution continued it became more violent, and struggles developed between competing Red Guard groups. By 1968 Mao began a new program of "sending youth down to the countryside." The ostensible goal was to learn about revolution from the peasants but it was also a way to get the Red Guards out of the cities once they had served Mao's ends.

Bourgeoisie. Marxist theory holds that history follows a definite series of stages of development (slavery, feudalism, capitalism, socialism, and communism); each is distinguished by a particular mode of economic production and the political dominance of a social class that controls that mode of production. The bourgeoisie are the dominant class in the capitalist stage, and they derive economic power from the exploitation of the working class. Marx based his staged theory of development on European experience, and the application of Marxism to China has always been problematic. Nonetheless, Marxist jargon came to be firmly imbedded in Chinese political discourse. According to the Maoist version, the bourgeoisie were an exploiting class and so being labeled bourgeoisie during the Maoist era brought discrimination and hardship. Thus, reversal of the ban on recruiting China's rising entrepreneur class into the CCP marks a major political turnaround.

Gang of Four. During the Cultural Revolution many CCP members rose to power rapidly by virtue of their personal loyalty to Mao and unstinting support of his policies. Many of these individuals fell from power just as rapidly after Mao's death. Most notorious among them was the "Gang of Four": Jiang Qing, Mao's third wife; Zhang Chunqiao, head of the CCP in Shanghai; Wang Hongwen, a party cadre from a textile factory; and Yao Wenyuan, a writer. All four were arrested in October of 1976. Jiang Qing was accused of being their ringleader and was charged with direct responsibility for the persecution of hundreds of party members. Although the Gang of Four members were far from innocent, their public trial and humiliation was as much a convenient venue for venting popular outrage at the excesses of the Cultural Revolution without directly tarnishing Mao Zedong's (and by association the CCP's) reputation. Mao was criticized in a posthumous party assessment of his career, but even so the party recognized that his lifelong accomplishments outweighed the errors of his last two decades.

Most-Favored-Nation. Under U.S. law, a trading partner that has been granted most-favored-nation (MFN) status automatically receives all the rights and privileges granted to the United States' most-favored nation. If the U.S. grants any additional rights or privileges to any other nation in the future, these automatically apply to all nations with most-favored-nation status. Since the normalization of relations between China and the U.S., the granting of most-favored-nation status has frequently become a domestic political issue in the U.S. Outspoken congressional critics of China's human rights record have frequently sought to link most-favored-nation status to improvements in human rights.

New Authoritarianism / Neo-conservatism. New authoritarianism has been described as "enlightened autocracy" to enforce economic development. Advocates of this approach cite the economic successes of Singapore, Taiwan, Hong Kong, and Korea—countries that share Confucian collectivism, family loyalty and frugality, as well as a patriarchal power structure—as evidence of the efficacy of new authoritarianism. In each of these countries economic modernization has taken precedence over political liberalization. While many anti-traditionalist intellectuals question the link between Confucian values and economic success, a more overtly nationalistic version of the theory, known as neo-conservatism, has gained new life after the suppression of the Tiananmen protests in 1989.

"Mass Line." The CCP developed the practice of the "mass line" during the early revolutionary period as method to gain popular support. The "mass line" approach was used to elicit information from the "masses" in order to create correct policies that would then be communicated back to the masses. After 1949 the CCP no longer faced political competition, but the practice of the mass line was continued, though in a more ritualized form. As the aftermath of the One Hundred Flowers Campaign showed, citizens could pay a high price for voicing opinions critical of CCP policy.

Review Questions

1. What were the three major goals of the Chinese Communist Party after 1949? How successful was the CCP in reaching its goals in the early years of the People's Republic of China?

2. Why does Dickson consider the end of the Cultural Revolution to be a turning point in the lives of many Chinese citizens? What was Mao's intent in launching the movement? What were its unintended consequences?

3. What do Rosen and Dickson identify as the sources of Chinese animosity toward the West? What are the political implications of rising Chinese nationalism in the 1990s? How does Shuisheng Zhao explain the rise of nationalist sentiments? How does the CCP manipulate these sentiments to its political advantage?

4. According to Andrew Walder, how was the student protest of 1989 in Beijing intellectually and politically different from earlier student-led protests? How did

it differ from the May Fourth Movement of the early twentieth century? What were the important foreign influences on the 1989 protest?

5. How have the CCP and its membership changed in the post-Mao era? According to Pearson, why has CCP recruitment of members of the emerging business class not guaranteed the development of democracy in China? What three factors have blunted a possible "democratic push" on the part of the business elite?

6. What standards can be used to evaluate the state of human rights in contemporary China? How has the human rights issue affected Sino-American relations? What issues have been raised in debate over how to pressure China to improve human rights. Do you agree or disagree with Nathan's evaluation of the policy of economic engagement?

7. In the post-Mao era, state-society relations have changed mostly for the better. How does the CCP exercise control in the post-Mao era? According to Dickson, what distinguishes Chinese civil society from that of other countries?

8. How has the CCP attempted to improve its standing at home and abroad since the Tiananmen crisis? How has the CCP attempted to broaden its base of support?

Society

This section examines both continuity and change between traditional and contemporary Chinese society. In addition to placing Chinese society in historical perspective, the readings and essay address the social consequences of economic reform in the post-Mao era, including changes in family patterns, rural-urban economic and social disparities, the revival of traditional cultural and religious practices, the status of women in contemporary society, and education.

Readings

21. "Family and Household," by Charlotte Ikels
22. "Home-Cured Tobacco—A Tale of Three Generations in a Chinese Village," by Daniel Wright
23. "How Come You Aren't Divorced Yet?" by Zhang Xinxin
24. "Human Rights Trends and Coercive Family Planning," by Martin K. Whyte
25. "McDonald's in Beijing," by Yunxiang Yan
26. "The *Fengshui* Resurgence in China," by Ole Bruun
27. "China's Catholics," by Richard Madsen
28. "Urban Spaces and Experiments in *Qigong*," by Nancy Chen
29. "Chinese Women in the 1990s," by Stanley Rosen
30. "Hey Coolie! – Local Migrant Labor," by Daniel Wright
31. "Second Class Citizens / Homosexuals in Beijing," by Ge Fei / Jin Ren
32. "Elementary Education," by Charlotte Ikels

Learning Objectives

To become acquainted with:
- the continuities and differences between traditional and modern Chinese society
- the role of the family in traditional and contemporary China

21

- the resurgence of traditional customs in rural China since 1978
- the revival of popular religions
- the appearance of Western-influenced consumption styles
- the problem of economic inequalities in post-Mao China

Overview

Over the course of the twentieth century China has experienced fundamental social changes, but these changes have not entirely supplanted "traditional" Chinese values. Martin Whyte's essay introduces the social institutions of traditional society and dilemmas that reformers faced in their efforts to change China. Interestingly, Whyte notes that the CCP has pursued the "age-old dream of Chinese statecraft"—a unified and orderly social hierarchy. Unlike the imperial rulers, however, the CCP commanded far greater resources and power, which they exploited in their efforts to reorganize society. By 1953, the year land reform formally concluded, the countryside had been drastically restructured, and the power of temple associations and lineages eliminated. In the cities the CCP gradually suppressed or absorbed autonomous social groups. Rural residents became members of CCP-controlled communes and most urban dwellers were organized into work units (*danwei*). Astoundingly, these changes were completed in less than a decade.

As a result of its reorganization of society, the CCP exercised unprecedented control over the daily of lives of the Chinese people. Unfortunately, this power was used to launch the disastrous mass movements of the Maoist era, such as the Great Leap Forward and the Cultural Revolution. By Mao's death, many Chinese were disillusioned with politics and ready for change. In response, Deng Xiaoping and other senior party leaders introduced market reforms, launched cultural exchanges with foreign countries, instituted legal reforms, rehabilitated millions of victims of the earlier political campaigns, and relaxed state controls over popular culture and individual behavior. The CCP continues to dominate society and will not tolerate organized opposition but political liberalization has accompanied economic reform and the material well-being of most Chinese people has improved over the past two decades.

Economic growth in the post-Mao era has improved the lives of the overwhelming majority of Chinese citizens, but there have been social costs. The articles by Charlotte Ikels and Zhang Xinxin reveal that attitudes toward the family and the institution of marriage have changed significantly during the period of economic reform. Divorce has become more common among China's upwardly mobile urban middle class. At the same time, Whyte's article on family planning shows that the patrilineal family system remains strong in rural areas where the preference for sons over daughters clashes with the government's one-child policy. Similarly, Wright's article, "Home-Cured Tobacco," reveals that traditional family values remain strong particularly in impoverished areas of the countryside.

Yunxiang Yan's article reveals how social change is in some cases spurred by outside influences, as illustrated by the proliferation of McDonald's restaurants. More important, as the state has relaxed its control over society, a greater diversity of popular customs has emerged. Religious practices and cultural traditions that many had assumed were eradicated during the Maoist period have been revived. Ole Bruun's piece on *fengshui*, the Chinese art of geomancy, demonstrates the tenacity of one traditional practice deemed "superstitious" in the early People's Republic. Christian churches established prior to 1949 have also demonstrated remarkable resiliency despite their long isolation. As Madsen's essay on Catholicism demonstrates, Catholic worship in China today enjoys an impressive resurgence. Although overt proselytizing remains illegal, Christianity has made inroads in recent years with the proliferation of "house churches." The question of religious revival certainly remains a complex issue. The current regime, like its dynastic predecessors, has been willing to tolerate religious diversity within prescribed boundaries but has ruthlessly attacked religious groups deemed politically threatening. In this light, the revival of *qigong* described by Nancy Chen presents a serious dilemma for the CCP. On the one hand, *qigong* practices have widely recognized physical and spiritual benefits; on the other hand, the influence of *qigong* masters over their followers has alarmed some within the government, leading to closer scrutiny and, in the case of the Falun Gong sect, a harsh crackdown.

The relaxation of control over Chinese society has reopened old debates about social equality. It has brought to the fore some previously unmentionable issues. Rosen's article addresses the paradox of the declining status of women during the period of economic reform and political liberalization. Since 1978 government control over internal migration has been relaxed, leading to a steadily expanding "floating population" of rural residents seeking work in the cities. Urban residents often disparage these "outsiders" and blame them for everything from increased crime to traffic jams, but Wright's article points to the economic and psychological hardships of the migrant laborer. Reports by Ge Fei and Jin Ren describe the increasingly visible underside of Chinese society. Although crime rates in China remain low by international standards, concern about increasing crime has lead to a series of highly publicized "strike hard" campaigns. Official persecution of homosexuality has lessened in recent decades but homosexuals still face discrimination in contemporary Chinese society.

Web Links

Resources on Chinese labor can be found at Hong Kong-based site *China Labour Bulletin* (http://www.china-labour.org.hk/iso/index.adp). This site provides up-to-date reports on Chinese unions and labor issues.

Another site, *Made in China,* focuses on labor in factories supplying products for U.S. companies: (http://www.nlcnet.org/report00/table_of_contents.htm).

On gender issues, *Human Rights in China* (http://iso.hrichina.org/iso/) has hundreds of reports that specifically address the status of women.

For articles on education and research, as well as links to related sites browse the English site of the Chinese Ministry of Education, *China Education and Research Network* (http://www.edu.cn/HomePage/english/index.shtml).

A number of websites are devoted to religion in China: *Society for the Study of Chinese Religions* (http://religion.rutgers.edu/SSCR/linksrel.html) provides an overview of resources on the Internet for the study of Chinese religions and also includes sources on Christianity in China. (Other sites on these issue, as well as public health can be found in **Online Resources** below.)

Documentary and Feature Film Suggestions

Given the pace of societal change in China over the past two decades, documentary films are at best snapshots of a work in progress. For example, three segments of the series *The Chinese*: *Caring*, *Marrying*, and *Mediating* capture the initial phase of the recent transformation quite well. *Mediating*, for example, recounts the efforts of a mediation committee to convince a young couple to reconsider their request for a divorce. But the events depicted in this film seem quaint when compared with the situations described in the reading, "How Come You Aren't Divorced Yet?" by Zhang Xinxin, and we can see how much has changed in urban China in the late twentieth century. *Marrying* depicts the rival of traditional wedding customs in rural China, but if it were made today, it would also report on the booming business of "wedding planners" in the cities. *Caring* has some unique footage of a mental hospital and prison, but the type of urban neighborhood depicted in this video is rapidly disappearing as cities undergo urban renewal.

Fortunately some recent documentaries give a picture of twenty-first-century China. Filmed in late 1999 and early 2000, *In Search of China* is one of best of these more recent efforts. The focus of the film is the transition from a planned to a market economy. The film shows how some individuals have prospered and others have failed under the new economic system. It also examines the lives of migrant laborers and the fate of several state-owned industries.

As several observers have noted, gender equality has suffered setbacks during reform era. Released in 1998, the two-part documentary *Women in China* provides a historical context for gender status as well as an update on the experiences of women since the launching of economic reforms.

A recent feature film that poignantly depicts the growing divide between urban and rural China is *Not One Less*. The film tells the story of a thirteen-year-old substitute primary school teacher in poor village who goes to the city in search of a runaway student. *The Story of Qiu Ju* tells of a peasant woman who launches a lawsuit against a village official. As the woman pursues her plaint, the film provides a telling portrait of the daunting layers of the Chinese bureaucracy. A normally hidden segment of contemporary Chinese society is depicted in *East Palace, West Palace,* which portrays gay life. The film explores the plight of a young homosexual as a means to address the broader issue of tension between an authoritarian regime and its diverse citizens.

Key Concepts

Lineage. A lineage is a corporate group that celebrates ritual unity and is based on demonstrated descent from a common ancestor. Throughout Chinese history lineages provided an important economic and social network for their individual members. The economic power of a lineage was based on its control of corporately owned landed estates. Lineage leaders often exercised enormous power over the lives of lineage members.

Communes. Prior to 1984, the commune was the basic administrative unit in rural China. There were over 50,000 communes in China in 1980. The average size was 15,000 people or 3,000 families. The commune was responsible for registry of births and marriages, postal services, and policing. Most communes also operated a clinic and a middle school. The reforms of the 1980s eliminated the communes as administrative units and replaced them with townships.

Class Labels. In the early 1950s each household in China was ascribed class label based on its pre-1949 socioeconomic status. Members of the revolutionary classes, such as peasants and workers, received good class labels, while former capitalists or landlords were considered bad elements. Such labels were particularly important during the process of land reform and later during the Cultural Revolution. For example, households designated as belonging to the landlord class had much of their land confiscated. Class labels were fixed so that future generations would continue to bear the stigma of belonging to a bad class, regardless of their actual socioeconomic situation. The system of class labels was finally abolished in 1979.

Danwei. In the 1950s all workplaces in urban China were organized into *danwei* or administrative units. The work unit served social, political, and economic functions. Each urban worker depended on his or her work unit for housing and social services. The work unit was also the center for political discussions of local and national issues.

"Floating Population." Since the 1980s a growing number of rural residents have migrated to China's more economically advanced urban areas in quest of better paying jobs. Estimates of this so-called floating population have ranged from 80 to 100 million. These migrants often retain close ties to their home townships, sending remittances that supplement rural incomes. The floating population commonly lacks access to social services and housing in the cities, and urban residents are frequently critical of them. While the floating population may place a strain on urban governments, and some of their number have taken to illegal activities, for the most part, migration has provided an important channel out of poverty for these workers and their families who remain behind in the countryside.

Guanxi. The Chinese term *guanxi* literally means "relationship," but in this context is best translated as "connections." The use of personal connections, such as kinship, school ties, and common places of origin, to obtain favors, bureaucratic advancement, or cement political ties has a long history in China.

Public Sphere / Civil Society. Public sphere refers to the existence of a separate realm that exists between the state and the private. Civil society is a concept referring to a multiplicity of substantially autonomous organizations and associations that arise to organize life within the public sphere.

Liberal and Statist Options. After the fall of the Qing dynasty (1644–1911) progressive Chinese intellectuals and politicians were united in their criticisms of Chinese tradition, but divided over the correct agenda for change. In his introductory essay, Martin Whyte contrasts what he terms the "liberal" and "statist" options. Those influenced by Western liberal tradition advocated the development of a modern state, a well-developed legal system, an extensive reliance on markets, and the freeing of individuals from the excessive demands of and loyalties to their families and other social groups. The "statist" option advocated many of the same goals, but its distinctive feature was the belief that individual freedom from group constraints was very dangerous, with social chaos the likely result. The proper solution was not to free individuals from the demands of families and personalistic groups, but to change the nature of these groups so that they would work to the benefit of society under the guidance of the state.

Qi. Qi, alternately translated as "configured energy" and "energetic configurations," is a vitalizing energy that is both universal and highly particular. *Qi* plays an important part in Chinese cosmological and metaphysical thought, as well as in traditional medicine. At times it means the spirit of life in living creatures; at other times it is the air or ether suffusing the universe. In some contexts it denotes the basic substance of all creation.

"Little Emperors." As compliance with the one-child policy has improved, the prospect of six adults, two sets of grandparents and two parents, doting on one child has raised concerns about a generation of spoiled children. The popular term for single children is "little emperors." Elementary school teachers

complain that the little emperors, accustomed to having all their desires met, lack discipline and expect teachers to comply with their every whim.

Review Questions

1. According to Martin Whyte, what are some of the salient features of traditional Chinese society? How have these traditional aspects of Chinese society continued to influence contemporary China?

2. Martin Whyte describes two modernization options, "liberal" and "statist," that were pursued during the Republican period (1912–1949). What were the major differences between these two options? How did the "statist" approach of the CCP resemble the social ideals of China's past?

3. What reasons do Daniel Wright's essays give for the persistence of poverty in rural China? How do Wright's portraits of rural China compare with the lifestyles of urban Chinese described in the articles by Ikels, Zhang, and Yan? How have urban and rural areas differed with regard to marriage and family planning?

4. Over the past two decades how has Chinese society been influence by the revival of traditional cultural practices and greater openness to foreign influences? How can you explain both the revival of *fengshui* and the widespread popularity of MacDonald's in contemporary China?

5. How has the collapse of faith in Marxist-Leninist-Mao Zedong thought and socialism in general fueled the search for alternative sources of meaning in Chinese society? What are some of the traditional alternatives? What alternatives have been imported from the West?

6. How have the economic reforms of the last two decades affected the status of women in China? How has the goal of gender equality been subordinated to economic growth?

7. What have been some of the negative impacts of the relaxation of social controls in Deng era? Describe some of the social problems that have become more visible in contemporary China?

8. What does Ikels' article on elementary education reveal about the impact of post-1978 reforms? How has funding for education changed in the post-Mao era? How do the changes in education exacerbate or ameliorate the gap between urban and rural China?

Economy

In addition to providing the historical background necessary to understanding the ongoing efforts to modernize the Chinese economy, this section examines the Maoist efforts at economic development and evaluates the current state of the Chinese economy. As the readings in this section reveal, despite some notable setbacks, overall the Chinese economy has improved steadily since 1949 and China's recent success is in fact the culmination of fifty years of ongoing economic growth.

Readings

33. "China 2020," The World Bank
34. "Is a Rich Man Happier than a Free Man?" by Cheng Le
35. "How to Reform a Planned Economy," by J. McMillan and B. Naughton
36. "Rural-Urban Divide: Economic Disparities in China," by John Knight and Lina Song
37. "Development in Chinese Corporate Finance," by Zhang Weijing

Learning Objectives

To become acquainted with:
- the historical antecedents of China's recent economic development
- the socialist industrialization of China's economy (1949–1978)
- the "Swiss cheese" economy of the first stage of reform (1978–1989)
- the reformulation of economic policy after the Tiananmen crisis (1989–1993)
- the impact of economic reform on rural China
- the challenges posed by China's entry into the World Trade Organization

Overview

Placing China's remarkable economic growth in historical perspective, Barry
Naughton's introductory essay notes that the unprecedented growth of China's
economy is the culmination of an ongoing process of development that began
fifty years ago. While economic growth has been most dramatic over the past
two decades, the transformation from an impoverished agrarian economy into a
prosperous semi-industrialized economy had already begun in the 1950s.
Despite the political struggles that marked the Maoist era, the commitment to
modernizing the Chinese economy was constant. Still, it was only after Mao's
death that Deng Xiaoping and other top leaders accepted the need to restructure
the economy. Since 1978 the Chinese economy has undergone dramatic changes,
including the dismantling of agricultural collectives and the introduction of
market reforms.

The hallmark of China's economic reforms has been pragmatic experimentation. The article by McMillan and Naughton reveals how Chinese leaders
displayed a remarkable degree of patience as they experimented with economic
reform avoiding the severe shocks of the "big-bang" approach adopted by
Eastern European governments. As Naughton notes in his introductory essay,
Chinese style reform created a "Swiss cheese" effect in which "holes" were
opened up to provide space for market activity within the structure of the old
planned economy. For roughly a decade this approach succeeded in producing
rapid growth that benefited a broad swath of Chinese society. As the World
Bank reports observe, this gradualist approach, coupled with political stability
and a high rate of savings, contributed greatly to China's early success.
Economic reform came to enjoy widespread popular support. Given the impact
of economic reforms at the grass-roots level in places such as the village
described in Cheng Li's article, it is no wonder the reform program met with
enthusiastic support. Huaxi Village had many advantages given its proximity to
Shanghai, but its story also points to the vast reservoir of entrepreneurial talent
bottled up in China prior to reform, as well as how successful businesses could
be built on institutions of the socialist era. At the same time, it also demonstrates
the renewed importance of traditional social units such as the family and village.

The Tiananmen crisis was an economic as well as a political watershed in
China's modern development. Politically, the CCP brutally served notice that it
would not tolerate organized political dissent nor would it entertain political

reform. It also provided an opportunity for conservative critics of the decade of economic experimentation to voice their opposition to the reform policies. After several years of economic retrenchment that eventually brought inflation under control, Deng Xiaoping's Southern Tour of 1992 broke the policy deadlock and set China back on the course of economic reform. In the ensuing decade, the Chinese economy has resumed its overall trend of steady growth, though at a slightly slower pace. Problems persist, however. Knight and Song's study of rural-urban migration reveals huge disparities between urban and rural living standards. Corporate finance and ownership reform are another trouble spot, and, as Weiying Zhang's article points out, solving these problems will be critical to China's continued economic success.

Web Links

Hong Kong Trade and Development Council (www.tdctrade.com) is a good source of up-to-date information about economic performance and policy in China. It also has links to thousands of other economy-related sites, many of which are in English.

Another useful site is *China: Economy, Industry, Business and Labor* (www.louisville.edu/library/ekstrom/govpubs/international/china/chinaecon.html).

For economic development, see the *World Bank East Asia: Social Policy and Governance*, (http://www.worldbank.org/eapsocial/), where you can find downloadable reports and statistical information. (See **Online Resources** for additional web resources related to the economy.)

Documentary and Feature Film Suggestions

The Chinese series includes three segments relevant to economics: *Living, Working,* and *Trading. Living* depicts a Chinese village after decollectivization but prior to the advances made with the expansion of Village and Township Enterprises described in the reading "Is a Rich Man Happier than a Free Man?" *Working* addresses the downsizing of state-owned enterprises, although that process had not yet begun when the film was made. *Trading* provides historical background to opening of China's economy in the post-Mao era and the cautious approach of foreign investors. A documentary made on this topic today would have to begin with the fact that China has recently surpassed the United States as the number one destination of foreign direct investment. A documentary mentioned above, *In Search of China*, focuses on the transition from a planned to a market economy. While the focus is often on individuals it also examines the fate of four different state-owned industries. Filmed in 1999 and early 2000, it provides a well-balanced presentation of winners and losers in the new economy. Economics rarely inspires feature films, but the recent picture, *Happy Times* is centered on a group of workers laid off from a state-owned enterprise. In addition to telling a touching and humorous story, the film also illustrates the circumstances of laid off workers who are too old to begin new careers. *Shower* follows a Beijing family that runs a traditional bathhouse and their community of customers when the bathhouse is slated for destruction in the name of progress.

Key Concepts

Commune System. Prior to the reforms of the 1980s the commune was the basic administrative unit in rural China. Economically, under the commune system, peasants were organized into production teams. Each team member was assigned work points, which were meant to measure both the quantity and quality of a team member's work. The reforms of the 1980s eliminated the communes as administrative units and replaced them with townships.

Contract or Household Responsibility System. Under the contract responsibility system each farming household was given a long-term lease on a plot of land. The land was still state-owned but each farming household had its own plot of land and sold any output in excess of the fixed state quota at free markets. Implementation of the household responsibility, which began in 1978, increased economic incentives for farming families and increased agricultural output. From 1978–1985 agricultural productivity increased 67 percent, creating wealth that was often invested in rural industry.

Special Economic Zone. In the early stages of economic reform, four "special economic zones" (SEZs) were set up along the south China coast. Within these zones special tax incentives and preferential treatment with regard to land, raw materials, customs regulations, labor contracts, and foreign currency controls were granted to foreign investors. SEZs contributed to economic development by bringing technology and investment to isolated areas while not threatening the government's ability to control the economy. This policy proved very successful and additional SEZs were gradually established during the 1980s.

State-owned Enterprise. State-owned enterprises (SOEs) are enterprises owned and administered by the Chinese government. The government appoints the management personnel, decides annual production targets, and determines wages and prices. In the post-Mao era, the total share of economic output produced by SOEs has steadily declined while the financial burden of these enterprises on the government has increased. According to a 1998 estimate, SOEs employed two-thirds of the industrial workforce and consumed two-thirds of China's investment resources, but produce only one-third of total output. Inefficient and grossly over-staffed, reform of the SOEs presents an ongoing challenge to China's economic leadership.

Deng Xiaoping's Southern Tour. In the aftermath of the Tiananmen crisis, Chinese reformers faced an equally important and related economic crisis. Rampant inflation and official corruption threatened to derail the economic reforms, and conservative elements in the CCP argued for rolling back reforms. It was under these circumstances that Deng Xiaoping undertook his "Southern Tour" of the Special Economic Zones, during which he gave a very public endorsement to accelerated economic reforms. Deng's public support was decisive in breaking a policy stalemate and resuming a new round of reforms.

Big Bang vs. Gradualist Economic Transitions. Western economists have used the terms "big bang" and "gradualist" to compare the different approaches that Eastern European countries and China have taken to economic reform. Orthodox economic opinion has favored the big-bang approach, which advocates a rapid transfer of state-owned enterprises to private ownership. Chinese reformers, on the other hand, have taken measured or gradualist steps to dismantle state-owned enterprises, preferring to invest in new firms run by profit-seeking entrepreneurs. So far this approach has proven successful. Non-state-owned enterprises in rural areas have been the most dynamic forces in the economic boom since 1984.

Township and Village Run Enterprises. Rural factories sprang up especially in villages close to urban markets, and their output soared until 1984. These so-called TVEs represented diverse activities, but most have remained "collectively owned" by the village community or government, or by the township government. TVEs outpaced economic growth in the overall economy and promoted competition.

Review Questions

1. What are the three simultaneous "transitions" that the Chinese economy is undergoing, according to Naughton? How are these transitions interrelated?

2. What are the "big-bang" and "gradualist" approaches to the transition from a planned to market economy? What model has China followed? And how has it been implemented?

3. What does the World Bank mean when it describes the process of economic reform in China since 1978 pragmatic and incremental? How has this approach contributed to China's economic success? What forces threaten to undermine China's future economic growth? What strengths favor continued economic development?

4. According to Naughton, what were the key characteristics of the market transition? What role did "township and village enterprises" (TVEs) play in the early stages of economic reform? Why have the initial stages of the transition been described as "reform without losers?"

5. What political and economic problems led to the reformulation of economic policy in 1993? What role did Deng Xiaoping play? What new policy adjustments did Zhu Rongji enact?

6. According to Knight and Song, what is the economic nature of the rural-urban divide in contemporary China? What are the positive affects of rural-urban migration?

7. What are the potential advantages to China's entry into the World Trade Organization (WTO)? What are the potential problems? Who stands to lose or gain by entry into WTO?

8. What problems does Weiying Zhang identify in "Chinese Corporate Finance"? How are state-owned enterprises financed? What is China's "over-indebted problem"?

Culture

This section examines elite and popular culture in the twentieth century. Historically, intellectuals have occupied an important and influential place in Chinese
society, and the state has played a major role in the shaping and monitoring of
both elite and popular culture. As the essay and readings demonstrate, the culture
of modern China is varied and complex, and has been intimately related to the
political struggles of the past century.

Readings

38. "Medicine," by Lu Xun
39. "Autumn Night," by Lu Xun
40. "Yan'an Talks," by Mao Zedong
41. "Sealed Off," by Zhang Ailing (Eileen Chang)
42. "The Unglovable Hands," by Zhang Shuli
43. "On the Other Side of the Stream," by Kong Jiesheng
44. "Responsibility," by Perry Link
45. "On the Road at 18," by Yu Hua
46. "Deathsong of the River," by Su Xiaokang and Wang Luxiang
47. "I Have Nothing," by Cui Jian
48. "Playing for Thrills," by Wang Shuo
49. "The Revolution of Resistance," by Geremie R. Barmé
50. "Fin de Siecle Splendor," by Zhu Tianwen
51. "Four Stanzas on Homesickness," by Yu Guangzhong

Learning Objectives

To become acquainted with:
- the traditional role of Chinese intellectuals
- the political and cultural contributions of intellectuals during the
  Republican period

- the Maoist interpretation of the relationship between culture and revolution
- the major trends in Chinese literature during the twentieth century
- the new varieties of cultural and artistic expression in the post-Mao era
- the changing sense of mission and responsibility on the part of Chinese intellectuals

Overview

As Professor Denton notes, the culture of modern China is "heterogeneous, multilayered, and closely intertwined with politics and shifting social identities." Traditionally, the idea of "culture" was associated solely with the literati, the highly educated social elite. Not only did the educated elites consider themselves the guardians of high culture, but, since the time of Confucius, they believed that government service was the duty of every intellectual. The link between intellectuals and the state was formalized during the Song dynasty (960–1279) when the civil service examination system became the primary method of recruiting government officials. Although cultural standards and the formal role of the intellectuals have undergone important transformations in the modern era, cultural institutions, artists, and scholars continue to occupy a central position in Chinese society. The intimate link between politics and culture remains an enduring aspect of Chinese civilization.

The advent of the aggressive commercial and military incursions of the West in the nineteenth century proved to be a cultural as well as an economic, military, and political challenge for China. By the end of the nineteenth century the role of the literatus and traditional views of culture began to change. The abolishment of the civil service examination, an institutional reform carried out in the name of modernization, severed the formal link between intellectuals and the state. With the May Fourth Movement of 1919, many Chinese intellectuals vociferously attacked traditional Confucian culture as a major obstacle to modernization. Intellectuals sought to refashion culture as a preliminary step toward transforming social and political institutions. As Professor Denton notes, while the goal was modernization and the destruction of tradition, "such a role for culture was fundamentally traditional."

Modern intellectuals also recognized the need to bridge the gap between elite and popular culture. For example, Liang Qichao (1873–1925) promoted literature written in the vernacular that addressed contemporary concerns. Equally important, he promoted the establishment of a commercial press and designed a more vernacular style of newspaper reportage. Many modern intellectuals were convinced that linguistic and literary reform was prerequisite to the transformation of Chinese society and polity. The work of Lu Xun (1881–1936), perhaps the most accomplished writer of this era, ranged from devastating critiques of the "national character" to poignantly personal reflections. Western cultural items available in China were diverse and influential during the Republican period (1912–1949). Translations of Western novels, biographies of famous national leaders, as well as treaties on law, capitalism, and evolutionary thought had a broad readership among educated Chinese. At the popular level, there was also a widespread interest in Western culture and especially the kind of escapist romances that came to be known as "Mandarin Ducks and Butterfly fiction."

By the late 1920s Marxism had also gained the attention of Chinese intellectuals. Marxist ideas had a potent influence on leftist writers, and eventually Mao Zedong's "Talks at the Yan'an Forum on Art and Literature" would define the political role of culture under the CCP. Mao made it clear that culture should serve the goals of revolution. In the 1920s and 1930s writers such as Zhang Ailing could still examine the private realm of the psyche as we see in her story "Sealed Off," but this sort of literature was vilified after 1949. From the inception of the PRC, politics dictated the direction of cultural production, and Mao's dictum that art and literature should "serve the masses" was firmly in place. Cultural works (literature, theater, artwork and music) were meant to depict workers, peasants, and soldiers and should be produced for that audience. Zhao Shuli's short story "The Unglovable Hands" demonstrates the post-1949 socialist realism that glorified poor peasants. Control over cultural expression reached absurd and tragic levels during the Cultural Revolution. Red Guards violently attacked anything smacking of "feudal" (traditional) and "bourgeois" (Western) culture. They destroyed religious artifacts and temples, family records and heirlooms, burned "offensive" books, and tortured hapless intellectuals, from village school teachers to government officials. Educated Chinese and Chinese professionals suffered grievously during the Cultural Revolution.

A new school of writing, "Wounds literature" emerged in the post-Mao era. Wounds literature portrays the personal suffering and political folly of the Cultural Revolution. The post-Mao leadership, many of whom suffered personally during the Cultural Revolution, actively promoted this type of literature.

Confronting the horrors of the Cultural Revolution was a form of social catharsis, but it also served the political goals of the post-Mao leadership. Kong Jiesheng's story depicts both the individual suffering and the irrational politics of the period. It depicts the hopelessness and loss of personal freedom that deeply scarred an entire generation. Prior to the Tiananmen crisis of 1989, Chinese intellectuals seemed poised to assume a more influential and independent political role. Avant-garde writers such as Yu Hua, author of *On the Road at 18*, pushed the limits of acceptable subject matter in literature. The controversial six-video documentary *Deathsong of the River* first aired in 1988 and attacked many of the cherished symbols of Chinese civilization and stirred debate in both cultural and political circles. Cui Jian, one of China's most famous rock stars, performed for the student protesters in Tiananmen and his song *I Have Nothing* became an anthem for the movement. After the brutal suppression of the protests in Beijing and other cities in June of 1989, state control of the media and cultural expression approached the levels of the Maoist era.

In the aftermath of Tiananmen, Chinese intellectuals faced new challenges. As Perry Link's essay indicates, many still felt the traditional sense of social responsibility. It was not until the decade of the 1990s that many of them began to questions this tradition and to view it as a source of authoritarianism. While many writers and artists grew more circumspect and avoided overt political messages, Geremie Barmé's article demonstrates that others took advantage of the flourishing new mass media and culture industry to voice their opinions. Writers such as Wang Shuo, author of *Playing for Thrills*, have felt free to experiment with new forms of expression. Wang's piece is an example of "punk literature" and examines the streetwise world of modern Beijing youth. A far cry from the exemplary characters of the Maoist era, Wang's punks drink, gamble, womanize, and mock conventional values. Punk literature may not carry an overt political message, but it can still be viewed as subversive. Finally, the works of Zhu Tianwen, a Chinese writer from Taiwan, and Yu Guangzhong, who grew up on the mainland but has lived in Taiwan and the U.S., remind us that Chinese culture is being shaped by "disparate" Chinese cultures, which, in turn, are part of a broader global culture.

Web Links

MCLC Resource Center (http://deall.ohio-state.edu/denton.2/biblio.htm) is the ultimate culture meta site. It provides articles, bibliographies and Iternet links related to literature, music, media, visual arts, education, online journals, institutions, e-texts, and translations.

Chinese-art.com (http://www.chinese-art.com/index_nonflash.htm) has images of both traditional and contemporary Chinese art, while the *Asian Film Connection* (http://www.usc.edu/isd/archives/asianfilm/china/) is an excellent site for information on current trends in the Chinese film industry. Asian Film Connection also includes sample course syllabi and useful links to film related websites.

The *Chinese Propaganda Poster Pages* (http://www.iisg.nl/~landsberger/), produced by Stefan Landsberger, is a delightful montage of over 1,300 propaganda posters.

For folk arts, handicrafts, and popular culture, the *China Experience: China Culture Index* (http://www.chinavista.com/experience/index.html) is a handy starting point. (See **Online Resources** for additional web resources related to culture.)

Documentary and Feature Film Suggestions

Documentary films on Culture often focus on an individual genre. Approaching culture from the broad concept of creativity, *Creating* from *The Chinese* series offers a more expansive view of Chinese culture. The film introduces painters, poets, writers, and musicians, many of whom suffered during the Cultural Revolution. By examining the impact of the Cultural Revolution the video addresses public role of the Chinese intellectual. It also attempts to demonstrate both the blending of Eastern and Western aesthetics, and the persistence of a distinctly Chinese approach to the arts. A recent restaging of *The Peony Pavilion*, an epic Chinese opera, is captured on the documentary video of the same name. Incorporating singing, dancing, acting, acrobatics, stilt walking, puppetry, pageantry, and martial arts, this is an exceptionally rich production that affords a sample of various types of performing arts.

Given the variety and richness of modern Chinese cinema, choosing a feature film to represent culture is no easy task. *Farewell My Concubine* tells the story of two Beijing opera performers against the backdrop of important historical events from the fall of the Qing dynasty to the Cultural Revolution. Among other things, the film depicts the harsh discipline of a pre-1949 Beijing opera troupe as well as the personal plights of performers during the Cultural Revolution. It also includes performances of scenes from a famous Beijing opera.

Key Concepts

May Fourth Movement. See **Geography and History** section.

Marxist materialism. During the 1920s Marxism began to exert a growing influence within cultural circles. Marxist intellectuals were critical of what they saw as the idealism of the May Fourth Movement's emphasis on changing popular consciousness through culture. Instead they assumed a materialist view of history that argues for real social transformation though changes in modes of production and class struggle. Despite their ultimate faith in materialism, radical intellectuals continued to recognize the important role of culture in historical development.

Mandarin Ducks and Butterflies Fiction. Mandarin ducks and butterflies fiction included sentimental love stories, detective fiction, comedies, and martial arts novels that tended to be iconoclastic and in favor of radical Westernization. This type of fiction became very popular during the Republican period (1912–1949). These works provided an escape from the drudgery of work and social problems.

"Seven Black Categories." The Cultural Revolution generated a unique political vocabulary. The "seven black categories" referred to politically suspect backgrounds: landlord, rich peasant, reactionary, bad element, rightist, traitor, and spy. (See also the **Society** section regarding class labels.) Other pejoratives used to dehumanized political enemies included terms like "snake spirits" and "cow ghosts."

Wounds Literature. Wounds literature is the work of a new generation of Chinese writers who came of age during the Cultural Revolution. Highly critical of the excesses of the Maoist era, their novels and stories represent a rigorous self-examination of and by people caught up in the excesses of the Cultural Revolution.

River Elegy. Released in 1988, *River Elegy* is a six-hour documentary that attacks symbols of traditional China, such as the Great Wall, dragons, the Yellow River. It portrays traditional Chinese civilization as backward and advocates following a Western model of development. The video was aired on Chinese television several times prior to the Tiananmen crisis of 1989.

Fifth-generation Film Directors. The "Fifth generation" refers to a group of young filmmakers who graduated from the 1982 class of the Beijing Film Academy. Their films created a new cinematic language that rejected the literary and narrative emphasis of mainstream films. Some of these artists have gone on to gain international acclaim, such as Chen Kaige, director of the film *Yellow Earth* and *Farewell my Concubine*, and Zhang Yimou, director of *Red Sorghum* and *To Live*.

"Punk Literature." Main characters are irreverent cynics who are unemployed and often engaged in illegal activities; they drink, gamble, and womanize, and speak in a Beijing street language. Punk literature mocks authority and socialist moral values.

Review Questions

1. According to Denton, how have modern Chinese intellectuals behaved in traditional ways since the late nineteenth century? What elements of tradition have survived in the modern era? In what ways have modern Chinese intellectuals broken with the past?

2. What do the writings of Lu Xun, Zhang Ailing, Kong Jiesheng, Zhao Shuli, Yu Hua, and Wang Shuo tell us about literary trends in twentieth-century China? How does each writer reflect the social and political climate of his or her times?

3. What were Mao Zedong's views on the relationship between literature and the arts, and revolution? How did this Maoist vision shape Chinese culture after 1949?

4. What "cultural" reforms took place during the Cultural Revolution? What new forms of cultural expression were approved during this period? What does

Wounds literature tell us about the experiences of artists and intellectuals during the Cultural Revolution? What are the political implications of Wounds literature?

5. What are some of the modern forms of cultural expression that have been popular in post-Mao China? What were some of the traditional cultural icons attacked in *River Elegy* and why? Why was *River Elegy* considered both culturally and politically controversial?

6. According to Perry Link, how has the traditional sense of social responsibility continued to influence contemporary intellectuals? According to Geremie Barmé, what dilemma faced the intelligentsia and cultural activists at the end of the twentieth century? How have the economic reforms of the past two decades affected the role of the intellectual in modern Chinese society?

7. What does the writing of Zhu Tianwen of Taiwan indicate about differences between cultural expression in Taiwan and the mainland? How does her writing compare with the works of her mainland Chinese contemporary Wang Shuo?

8. How have economic reforms affected Chinese cultural institutions? How has the "commercial tide" of the 1990s changed the role of culture in modern China?

Future Trends

Throughout this volume the readings have examined the influence of China's past on the ongoing struggle to modernize. This section speculates on future developments, considering economic, political, and social issues as well as Sino-American relations.

Readings

Learning Objectives

To become acquainted with:
- the next generation of Chinese leaders
- the impact of the Internet on Chinese society
- the challenges posed by ongoing efforts to modernize and globalize the economy
- the rise of nationalism in contemporary China
- the prospects for democratization in China

Overview

In the past, Western observers have not had much success in predicting China's future. For example, the Cultural Revolution, which had such an enormous impact on Chinese society, took most outside observers by surprise. Throughout the 1980s American observers almost universally applauded China's political and economic reforms. The brutal crackdown on political dissent on June 4, 1989, in response to the Tiananmen Square protests stunned the world and cast a pall over Sino-American relations. Despite these tragic events however, the CCP eventually resumed its program of economic reform. Professor Dickson notes that over past twenty years the CCP has abandoned the key policies and institutions of the Maoist era. Collective farms have been dissolved in favor of contracts between the state and private family farmers. State-owned industries are slowly being dismantled in favor of private entrepreneurship. Legal reforms protect private property rights. Ideological indoctrination has largely been abandoned and the Internet, satellite television, and a burgeoning private commercial press are undermining state-control of information. A rising standard of living and relaxation of the political atmosphere seem to have placated the majority of the Chinese people. In the face of all these changes, what endures more than fifty of years after the founding of the People's Republic of China, is the CCP itself.

Despite the extensive economic, legal, and administrative reforms of the past two decades, the CCP strictly maintains its monopoly on political power. But, as material well-being has replaced political ideology as the standard of legitimacy, the CCP has staked its future on continued economic development. Balancing the demands of sustaining economic development and ensuring political survival, the party has undertaken some seemingly contradictory actions. On the one hand, it has targeted successful businessmen for recruitment. On the other hand, it has cracked down hard on the Chinese Democratic Party. It remains to be seen if China's farmers, workers, and businesspeople will continue to accept political repression as the price for economic prosperity. The CCP faces many difficult choices in order to sustain economic growth and curtail official corruption. For example, the necessary but painful downsizing of state-owned enterprises has left many workers unemployed. Similarly, official corruption threatens social stability as well as the internal cohesion of the party. Finally, the CCP's abandonment of ideology in favor of material incentives has left a philosophical void that traditional and foreign religions have filled. For the most part the CCP has tolerated the revival of religious practice, but when the party has viewed a religion as politically threatening, as in the case of Falun Gong, it has not hesitated to punish its members. Other problems the CCP must face include the challenge of the Internet, environmental pollution from rapid economic growth, increased foreign competition after entry into the World Trade

Organization, and the resolution of the status of Taiwan. These matters will pose substantial domestic and international challenges for China's future leaders.

As China enters the twentieth-first century it has seen another genera-tional change in leadership. Susan Lawrence's article "handicaps" five of the front runners in China's new generation of leaders. It seems likely that China's next leaders will support the primacy of the CCP and market-oriented economic reform. Like the outgoing leadership, the successors are college-educated party bureaucrats who lived through the turmoil of the Cultural Revolution as well as two decades of mostly successful economic reform. As Oksenberg, Swain, and Lynch discuss in their essay, this new leadership will face a plethora of issues from the environment to integration into the world economic system. Their article notes that future leaders will face a vastly different polity and society. Policy implementation will be complicated by the fact that individuals have more geographical and occupational freedom and government authority is more decentralized. What role the military will play in politics is also uncertain, but all successful leaders since 1949 have had to cultivate support within the armed services. Oksenberg, Swain, and Lynch also note the "bewildering array of contradictions" that characterizes contemporary Chinese society including cosmo-politanism and nativism, internationalism and nationalism, and materialism and spiritualism.

As noted in Professor Naughton's introductory essay to the Economy section, China is in the midst of transformation into a modern information economy. The Internet has had a deep impact on Chinese society. While others have looked at the potential political impact of a loosely monitored information network, John Pomfret's article looks at the more mundane consequences of the Internet, such as finding jobs, meeting people, and buying products. At least in modernized urban areas, the Internet has changed people's lives in ways that would be very familiar to Americans. On the negative side, access to the Internet has also exacerbated the urban-rural divide within Chinese society. Politically, it remains to be seen if the Internet will become a tool for democratizing China. Martin Whyte's article evaluates the prospects for future of democratization. Professor Whyte rebuts many of the historical factors that have been cited as obstacles to democratization and enumerates a number of factors that favor its development. The final piece in the volume is by one of China's most renowned dissidents, Wei Jingsheng. Wei was active during the Democracy Wall Movement of 1978–1979. After serving nearly two decades in prison, he was released in

1997 and went into exile in the United States. When China's leaders called for the "Four Modernizations" in industry, agriculture, national defense, and science and technology, Wei boldly suggested a fifth modernization—democracy. This article stands as an eloquent testament to a dream still unfulfilled.

Key Concepts

Central Discipline Inspection Commission is a special body whose mission is to investigate and punish corruption in the party, government, and the military. As local autonomy has grown, so has corruption in provincial and local governments. Understaffed and underfunded, this commission has not been able to stem the tide of official greed.

"*House Churches.*" Under Chinese law, all religious organizations must register with the Ministry of Civil Affairs. House churches refer to small, unregistered Christian congregations that usually meet in the homes of members.

Review Questions

1. According to Bruce Dickson, what changes has the CCP undergone in the post-Mao era? How has the role of the CCP changed? How has it remained the same?

2. What are the potential sources of future political and social unrest in China, according to Dickson? Why does the state view some religious movements as politically threatening?

3. What have been the consequences of the decentralization of political authority during the reform era? How has decentralization exacerbated the problem of official corruption?

4. According to Susan Lawrence's article, what qualifications and traits do the future leaders of China share? How is this new generation of leaders likely to differ from their predecessors? What new problems will the next generation of leaders face in their quest to modernize China?

5. What impact has the Internet had on the daily lives of people in China? What has limited this impact? How will the Internet influence China's economic, social, and political development?

6. According to Oksenberg, Swain, and Lynch, what are the major domestic concerns that will challenge the next generation of China's leaders? What contradictory social trends will threaten social and political stability in the twenty-first century? What political quandaries will Chinese leaders face in the twenty-first century?

7. What historical and sociological factors have been cited as obstacles to China's future democratization? How does Martin Whyte's refute these arguments? What socioeconomic factors have been mentioned as potential barriers to democratization? According to Whyte, what forces favor democratization?

8. What does Wei Jingsheng mean by "true democracy?" What does Wei believe the Chinese people must do in order to achieve political reform?

Essay / Discussion Questions

1. How did the forces of "feudalism" and "imperialism" shape China's pursuit of modernization in the late nineteenth and twentieth centuries?

Suggested guidelines:

    a. Consider the meaning of these concepts during the late Qing referring to:

- Buoye's *Introduction* to **Geography and History**
- Fairbank discussion of feudalism and imperialism (reading 4)
- Cohen's exploration of domestic unrest and foreign intervention (reading 6)

    b. Consider competing approaches to modernization after the fall of the Qing referring to:

- Schwarcz's discussion of intellectuals and the state in the May Fourth Era (reading 7)
- Whyte's discussion of the liberal and statist options for modernization in the *Introduction* to **Society**

    c. Consider the persistence and reemergence of tradition in post-Mao China referring to:

- Denton's discussion of the political role of intellectual in the *Introduction* to the **Culture** section
- Mao's views on art and literature (reading 40)
- Link's article on the dilemmas faced by contemporary intellectuals (reading 44)
- Dickson's discussion of the reemergence of feudal influences in his *Introduction* to the **Future** section

2. What are some of the environmental and ecological concerns associated with China's economic modernization?

    Suggested guidelines:

a. Consider China's environment history and impact of two decades of economic growth referring to:

- McNeil's reading on environmental history (reading 1)
- Naughton's *Introduction* to the **Economy** section
- Oksenberg et al. discussion of the Chinese future (reading 54)

3. How have the historic economic, political and cultural disparities between China's rural and urban populations continued to influence the country's development in the modern era?

Suggested guidelines:

a. Consider the importance of rural uprisings in China referring to:

- Buoye's *Introduction* to the **History** section the Taiping Rebellion (reading 5)
- Mao's report on the peasant movement in Hunan in 1927 (reading 9)

b. Consider political and economic reform in rural China after 1949 referring to:

- White's article on village elections (reading 19)
- Knight and Song's essay on economic disparities (reading 36)
- Wright's report on migrant labor (reading 30)

4. How has religion continued to serve important social and political functions in modern China?

Suggested guidelines:

a. Consider the historical role of religion in political movements referring to:

- Cohen's examination of the Boxer Uprising (reading 6)
- the Taiping challenge to Confucian orthodoxy (reading 5)

b. Consider the reemergence of religious beliefs in contemporary China referring to:

- Madsen's article on Chinese Catholics
- Chen's discussion of the *qigong* in contemporary urban China
- Eckholm's report on Falun Gong

5. To what extent has the family remained an enduring social and economic institution in China?

Suggested guidelines:

a. Consider the importance in economic development referring to:

- Li's study on rural enterprise (reading 34)
- Wright's report on one family in a poor village (reading 22)

b. Consider the changing status of women in modern society referring to:
- Zhang's story of a young woman in 1930s Shanghai (reading 41)
- Rosen's analysis of women in the 1990s (reading 29)

c. Consider changing family values in contemporary China referring to:
- Kang's story of one family's ordeal during the Cultural Revolution (reading 42)
- Ikel's study urban households in Guangzhou (reading 21)
- Zhang's report on divorce in urban China (reading 23)

6. What major political issues face the CCP as China enters the twenty-first century?

Suggested guidelines:

a. Consider the issues of human rights referring to:
- Walder's assessment of the legacy of Tiananmen (reading 13)
- Nathan's discussion of human rights in China (reading 15)

b. Consider internal problems in the CCP referring to:
- Miles article on political corruption (reading 20)
- Rosen's discussion of post-Tiananmen politics (reading 14)
- Lawrence's analysis of China's future leaders (reading 52)

c. Consider the prospects for future democratization referring to:
- Pearson's study of the emerging business class (reading 18)
- Whyte's speculation on the future prospects for democracy (reading 55)
- Wei's discuss of the "fifth modernization" (reading 56)

d. Consider the future of Sino-American relations referring to:
- historical Sino-American misunderstandings (readings 11 and 12)
- Zhao's examination of rising Chinese nationalism (reading 16)
- Oksenberg et al.'s consideration of future foreign policy (reading 54)

Online Resources

There is a dizzying array of resources for teaching about China available on the web. In addition to several "meta sites" that provide a seemingly endless number of links, there are numerous narrowly focused sites that provide information on everything from acupuncture to the Zhou dynasty. The purpose of this section is to provide a brief overview of some of the sites that will be useful for teaching an introductory level course on contemporary China. This list is by no means exhaustive. As one quickly learns while surfing the web for teaching resources, the quality, maintenance, and durability of sites can be quite variable. Some sites are individual labors of love while others are poorly designed or blatantly commercial. I have attempted here to provide an annotated list of the more helpful sites. Any text appearing in quotes was taken directly the website's self-description. References to sites that offer relevant information are also included in each section of the study guide.

In addition to a good bit of indiscriminate surfing, a most valuable source for information on internet resources was "Web Gleanings" by Judith Ames, a regular column of *Education About Asia* (http://www.aasianst.org/eaa-toc.htm). *Education About Asia* is published three times per year by the Association for Asian Studies. As the title indicates the scope of this publication is broad but it often includes features, essays, book and film reviews, and resources related to China. Another useful source is "Asia Resources on the World Wide Web," by Richard Lum, a column that appears in the *Asian Studies Newsletter* (http://www.aasianst.org/catalog/nl.htm). The *Asian Studies Newsletter* is also published by the Association of Asian Studies. These two columns provide brief description of sites and are essential sources for keeping abreast of the unrelenting proliferation of websites. Finally, I must issue a disclaimer and an apology. Undoubtedly, by the time this study guide goes to press new sites will be created and old ones will disappear into cyber heaven. I apologize in advance to the creators of sites that I may have overlooked or that may have appeared since this guide went to press.

Meta Sites

The sites listed below directly or indirectly provide links to seemingly every conceivable website on China. There is some overlap but one would be wise to sample all of them. As noted above, things change quickly on the web and some sites are better at keeping links up-to-date. When I visited these sites in the fall of 2002, I sometimes encountered outdated links. Since these sites are omnifarious, no brief description can do them justice. It is best to start surfing!

Association of Asian Studies Asia Resources on the World Wide Web, China
http://www.aasianst.org/wwwchina.htm

Internet Guide for Chinese Studies, Institute of Chinese Studies, Heidelberg University
http://sun.sino.uni-heidelberg.de/igcs/

Marjorie Chan's China Links
http://www.deall.ohio-state.edu/chan.9/c-links.htm

Curriculum and Teaching

Anyone designing an entry-level course on China will find the websites listed below essential. Taken together these sites provide comprehensive teaching materials, lesson plans, and resource links.

A Visual Sourcebook of Chinese Civilization
http://depts.washington.edu/chinaciv/ ˙
      The Visual Sourcebook of Chinese Civilization was designed to "add to the material teachers can use to help their students understand Chinese history, culture, and society." The strength of this site is its use of images. These images illustrate ten subject areas: geography, archaeology, religion, calligraphy, military technology, painting, homes, gardens, clothing and the graphic arts. The coverage spans prehistory to the twentieth century.

Asia for Educators
http://afe.easia.columbia.edu/
 This site is part of the Columbia University East Asian Curriculum Projects, and it contains information on China and Japan. The subject areas are organized as follows: art, language, literature, religion and philosophy, geography, population, society and culture, economy and trade, foreign policy and defense, government and politics, inventions/ideas, history to 1800, and history, 1800 to the present. The site provides overviews of important topics, primary sources, articles, and links to related sites.

Five College Center for East Asian Studies (FCCEAS) (Amherst, Hampshire, Mount Holyoke, and Smith Colleges, and the University of Massachusetts, Amherst)
http://www.smith.edu/fcceas/links.html
 FCCEAS was established "to support, encourage, and improve the teaching of East Asian cultures in elementary, middle, and secondary schools and two-year colleges in New England." This site has a list of meta sites that are useful for teachers developing courses on China and Asia.

China Bibliography and Collections of Resources
http://hua.umf.maine.edu/China/bibtxt2.html
 Created by Marilyn Shea, this site has particularly useful bibliographic information on a number of selected topics ranging from Buddhism to an especially good listing of works on women in Chinese history.

Research Aids
http://www.let.leidenuniv.nl/bth/index.html
 Created by Barend ter Haar, this website includes bibliographies on protest, violence, and literacy, and religion.

Asian Educational Media
http://www.aems.uiuc.edu/index.las
 The Center for East Asian and Pacific Studies at the University of Illinois Urbana-Champaign created this website to help instructors locate media materials, including documentary films, feature films, CD-ROMs, and slide units. Searches on this site can be limited by region, media type, and audience level.

Country Profiles and Government Websites

The sites included in this category provide a wide range of basic information on the economy, government, language, culture, news, travel, and business. These sites are generally kept up-to-date.

China Internet Information Center
http://www.china.org.cn/english/index.htm
This is an official PRC government website. It is especially good for the official view on current events, statistics, and government white papers.

World Fact Book (CIA)
http://www.odci.gov/cia/publications/factbook/geos/ch.html
This U.S. Central Intelligence Agency site provides a succinct profile of every country in the world. It is handy for quick reference and is designed for making quick comparisons between countries.

The Asia Society
http://www.asiasource.org/
The Asia Society is a nonprofit educational institution "dedicated to fostering understanding of Asia and communication between Americans and the peoples of Asia and the Pacific." This site is an excellent starting point for China, and all other Asian countries. A very good source for the latest news, it also includes a database of specialists.

Embassy of the People's Republic of China
http://www.china-embassy.org/eng/
This official government website provides information about China, Sino-American relations, and the PRC embassy, as well as links to a variety of specialized Chinese government websites.

U. S. State Department
http://www.state.gov/www/current/debate/china.html
This website contains U.S. State Department policy statements and country reports on commerce, military capabilities, human rights, and other topics.

China National Space Administration
http://www.cnsa.gov.cn/main_e.asp

This official website of the Chinese National Space administration contains information on China's aerospace policy and space program.

GEOGRAPHY AND HISTORY

Meta Site

WWW-VL: History: China
http://www.ukans.edu/history/VL/east_asia/china.html

Part of World Wide Web Virtual Library, this meta site is an essential starting point for the geography and history of China. It provides many useful links to historical maps, images, bibliographies, primary texts, and overviews of Chinese history.

Maps

Perry-Castañeda Library Map Collection University of Texas
http://www.lib.utexas.edu/maps/china.html

An excellent source for maps of any country, this site provides detailed, thematic, and historical maps of China.

China Historical GIS, Harvard-Yenching Institute
http://www.fas.harvard.edu/~chgis/

Currently this site provides county-level geographic information system (GIS) maps for Qing (1820) and modern China (1990), and GIS datasets. This is a large-scale collaborative project with ambitious plans for expansion. Future plans call for establishing "a database of historical administrative units for different periods in Chinese history," and providing "a base GIS platform for researchers to use for spatial analysis, temporal statistical modeling, and representation of selected historical units as digital maps."

Maps of China

http://emuseum.mnsu.edu/prehistory/china/map/map.html

The E-Museum at Minnesota State University maintains this site, which includes a very handy set of historical maps.

China in Time and Space (CITAS)

http://citas.csde.washington.edu/

China in Time and Space (CITAS) is a project to create and maintain databases of spatially and temporally referenced data on China.

Environment

China New Energy Network

http://www.newenergy.org.cn/english/index.asp

The China New Energy Network is a "nonprofit professional information network system constructed by Guangzhou Institute of Energy Conversion, Chinese Academy of Sciences." It contains information and articles about alternative energy research and projects in China, with timely news updates.

Can China Feed Itself?

http://www.iiasa.ac.at/Research/LUC/ChinaFood/index_m.htm

This site contains a report by International Institute for Applied Systems Analysis. In addition to the narrative report, the site includes datasets, maps, and graphs as well as links to related sites.

World Bank Pollution Index

http://www.worldbank.org/nipr/data/china/status.htm

NIPR (New Ideas in Pollution Regulation) is the "primary source for materials produced by the World Bank's Economics of Industrial Pollution Control Research Project." This link provides a downloadable dataset on air quality in Chinese cites. It also includes abstracts of articles based on this dataset.

International Fund for China's Environment

http://www.ifce.org/

International Fund for China's Environment is a nonprofit non-government organization (NGO) that was founded by "a group of concerned scientists and professionals in 1996." The site provides information on conservation efforts in China.

International Rivers Network (IRN)
http://www.irn.org/programs/threeg/
　　INR is "a nonprofit all-volunteer organization of activists experienced in fighting economically, environmentally, and socially unsound river intervention projects." This site contains information and news related to the Three Gorges Project in China.

Flora of China
http://flora.huh.harvard.edu/china/
The Flora of China website seeks to describe and document the nearly 30,000 plant species in China. Some of the information is rather technical, but the site includes images and maps that will be of interest to everyone.

National Minorities

Languages of China
http://www.ethnologue.com/show_country.asp?name=China
　　This site has a complete list and brief description of all "spoken living languages" in China. The site is a component of the *Ethnologue: Languages of the World* website.

Ethnic Minorities
http://www.china.org.cn/e-groups/shaoshu/index.htm
　　The China Internet Information Center, an official government website provides basic information on each of China's minority nationalities.

History

Internet East Asian History Sourcebook
http://www.fordham.edu/halsall/eastasia/eastasiasbook.html
　　Created by Paul Halsall, this site includes links to primary and secondary texts, many images, and other web links related to East Asian and Chinese history. Materials cover early history through modern times. This is a very useful site for an introductory course on Chinese culture and history.

China History
http://www.usc.edu/isd/locations/ssh/eastasian/toqing.htm
　　This site includes overviews, documents, images, bibliographies and web links for Chinese history from the "Dawn of Time" through the Ming dynasty.

Yi-Luo River Archaeological Survey
http://www.latrobe.edu.au/archaeology/research/survey/index.htm
　　Chronicling an ongoing archaeological survey, this site provides images and reports on a study of the "dynamics of regional settlement patterns covering the entire Neolithic and Three Dynasties (c. 6500–200 B.C.) eras.

Women in Chinese History
http://hua.umf.maine.edu/China/womtxt.html
　　This site contains Marilyn Shea's extensive bibliography on women's history.

Portraits of Chinese Emperors
http://www.chinapage.com/emperor.html
　　This site has links to portraits of Chinese emperors from the Tang through Qing.

Philosophy

Warring States Project
http://www.umass.edu/wsp/
　　This site is devoted to Warring States period, "China's classical Golden Age of thought and political achievement." It is a scholarly site that offers a new perspective on early China.

Chad Hansen's Chinese Philosophy Pages
http://www.hku.hk/philodep/ch/
　　The interpretive theory behind this website takes "Daoism as the philosophical center." In addition to its innovative interpretive approach, the site also contains related writings of the Confucian, Mohist, and Legalist schools. It is an impressive individual effort.

Essential Readings on Chinese Philosophy
http://faculty.vassar.edu/brvannor/bibliography.html
    Created by Bryan W. Van Norden, this site includes "only works that are essential reading on particular topics." Works that are appropriate for beginners are marked for the user's convenience.

The Cult of Confucius: Images of the Temple of Culture
http://www.hamilton.edu/academics/Asian/TempleCulture.html
    Created by Thomas Wilson, this site presents a chronology of the "changing status of Confucianism as official teaching." It includes texts, commentary, and photos of Confucian temples.

POLITICS

Current Events

Inside China Today
http://www.einnews.com/china/
    This site provides breaking news on China and more than 200 other countries.

People's Daily
http://english.peopledaily.com.cn/
    For the official PRC view on current events at home and abroad, this link will take you to the English language site of the *People's Daily*.

Political Leadership

China Leadership Monitor
http://www.chinaleadershipmonitor.org/
    Supported by the Hoover Institution at Stanford University, the *China Leadership Monitor* is an electronic journal that offers "assessments of trends in Chinese leadership politics and policy."

Leadership Transition
http://taiwansecurity.org/TSR-CNL.htm
This link on the *Taiwan Security Research* website (see also below, **Taiwan**) compiles news reports and press accounts related to PRC leadership. It appears to be updated regularly.

Human Rights

Human Rights in China
http://iso.hrichina.org/iso/
The organization Human Rights in China describes itself as "an international non-governmental organization founded by Chinese scientists and scholars." Its goals include educating, advocating and monitoring human rights in China. It provides web links, press releases, and downloadable reports.

Chinese Human Rights Web
http://www.chinesehumanrightsreader.org
Chinese Human Rights Web is "devoted to informed discussion of both historical and contemporary human rights issues." The site includes texts, bibliography, government documents, and web links.

Amnesty International: China
http://web.amnesty.org/ai.nsf/Index/ASA170542002?OpenDocument&of=COU NTRIES\CHINA
Amnesty International issues annual reports on human rights in China and also provides reports on executions, political and religious repression, and other types of human rights violations.

International Relations

National Committee on U.S.-China Relations
http://www.ncuscr.org/index.htm
The National Committee on U.S.-China Relations is a nonprofit educational organization that "encourages understanding of China and the United States between citizens of both countries." This site has full texts of speeches by American and Chinese officials and scholars and is a good source

for information on scholarly and cultural exchanges, including student and teacher exchanges.

Archive Resources on U.S.-China Relations
http://www.gwu.edu/~nsarchiv/NSAEBB/NSAEBB41/
This link will take you to the National Security Archives. The site provides declassified U.S. government documents and includes a report on reconnaissance flights and Sino-American relations. Be sure to check the side bar on the right for additional reports and declassified U.S. government documents related to Sino-American relations.

Taiwan

Taiwan Security Research
http://taiwansecurity.org/TSR-PRC.htm
This site is "an academic and non-governmental website." It includes information on current events related to Taiwan's security, including news from the People's Republic of China. It draws on English-language press reports, academic papers and official policy statements. A number of leading China experts have praised this site.

Taiwan Online
http://www.roc-taiwan.org/
This is the official website of the Government Information Office of the Republic of China in Taipei. It includes basic information about Taiwan and daily news updates.

New Taiwan
http://www.taiwandc.org/index.html
This site includes links to the Democratic Progressive Party (DDP), and Formosan Association for Public Affairs (FAPA), Center for Taiwan International Relations (CTIR), organizations that favor independence for Taiwan.

Military

Chinese Military Power
http://www.comw.org/cmp/index.html

The Project on Defense Alternatives (PDA) sponsors this website which provides "a compendium of online resources about Chinese military policy and capabilities." The site also has links to other websites that evaluate Chinese military power.

Tiananmen Crisis of 1989

The Gate of Heavenly Peace
http://www.tsquare.tv/

The Long Bow Group, makers of awarding winning documentaries on China, have created this comprehensive website on the 1989 Tiananmen crisis. The site features historical background of the crisis, video clips, and transcripts of the documentary, and additional readings and web links.

Tiananmen Square
http://www.gwu.edu/~nsarchiv/NSAEBB/NSAEBB16/index.html

This site of the National Security Archives contains declassified government documents and a narrative history of the Tiananmen Square crisis.

Tiananmen, April-June 1989
http://www.christusrex.org/www1/sdc/tiananmen.html

This site includes a gallery of graphic and even shocking photos of the Tiananmen movement and its bloody suppression.

Law

Internet Chinese Legal Research Center
http://ls.wustl.edu/Chinalaw/

Created by Wei Luo, this site has links to legal resources related to research on China, Taiwan, and Hong Kong law.

China Law
http://www.qis.net/chinalaw/lawtran1.htm

China Law is based at the University of Maryland Law School. It provides information about the laws and the legal systems of "greater China." Greater China includes, the People's Republic of China and the Republic of

China on Taiwan. The site contains translations of laws as well as articles on various topics.

SOCIETY

Bibliographies

Social Forces
http://hua.umf.maine.edu/China/social.html
    This is a link to another excellent bibliography on Marilyn Shea's *China Bibliography and Collections of Resources* website.

Violence (Barend ter Haar)
http://www.let.leidenuniv.nl/bth/violence.htm
    This site contains Barend ter Haar's extensive bibliography on violence in Chinese society.

Labor

China Labour Bulletin
http://www.china-labour.org.hk/iso/index.adp
    This Hong Kong-based website provides up-to-date reports on Chinese unions and labor issues. Topics include health and safety, child labor, women workers, labor law, labor disputes, and economic reform.

China Labor Watch
http://www.chinalaborwatch.org/
    China Labor Watch (CLW) "is devoted to improving Chinese workers' working and living conditions." It includes reports, articles, labor laws, and interviews with Chinese workers.

Made in China
http://www.nlcnet.org/report00/table_of_contents.htm
    This site contains a detailed report on U.S. companies and worker rights in China, by National Labor Committee (NLC). Among other things the report details the wages and working conditions of Chinese workers employed by American corporations.

Labor Issues

http://www.china-un.ch/eng/c4389.html

This site of the Permanent Mission of the PRC at the United Nations Office in Geneva provides the official view on labor issues.

Education

China Education and Research Network

http://www.edu.cn/HomePage/english/index.shtml

This English language website of the PRC Ministry of Education contains articles on education and research as well as links to other relevant sites.

Literacy

http://www.let.leidenuniv.nl/bth/literacy.htm

This site contains another excellent bibliography prepared by Barend ter Haar. The coverage ranges from the earliest forms of writing to modern times.

Women

Human Rights in China

http://iso.hrichina.org/iso/

This site contains over one hundred reports from Human Rights in China (see above, **Politics**) regarding the status of Chinese women. Search the site using the keyword "women."

Village Works: Photographs by Women in China's Yunnan Province

http://www.wellesley.edu/DavisMuseum/VillageWorks/introduction.html

This site contains an exhibition of photos taken by Chinese women in Yunnan Province from 1992–1993. The project was sponsored by the Ford Foundation and it provides a unique view of rural China from the perspective of rural Chinese women. Be sure to click on the exhibition link to view the photos.

Ethnography and Video: Researching Women in China's Floating Population

http://wwwsshe.murdoch.edu.au/intersections/back_issues/tampt1.html

Tamara Jacka and Josko Petkovic have created this site which contains a report on women in the floating population that includes seven video clips of interviews from their 1995 fieldwork.

Women of China
http://www.womenofchina.com.cn/

This is the website of the contemporary women's magazine, *Women of China*. There are bilingual articles though some reports and essays appear in Chinese only.

Iron Women and Foxy Ladies
http://www.iisg.nl/~landsberger/iron.html

From Stefan Landsberger's propaganda poster website (see below, **Culture**), these posters vividly present the changing official views of the role of Chinese women.

Women in Chinese History
http://hua.umf.maine.edu/China/womtxt.html

This site contains an extensive bibliography (see above, **History**).

Religion

Society for the Study of Chinese Religions
http://religion.rutgers.edu/SSCR/linksrel.html

This meta site provides an overview of resources on the Internet for the study of religion in China, including ancestor worship, shamanism, Buddhism, Daoism, Islam and Christianity.

Bibliography of Western Language Publications on Chinese Popular Religion
http://web.missouri.edu/~religpc/bibliography_CPR.html

Philip Clart maintains this site that includes a growing bibliography of twenty topics related to popular religion.

Taoism Information Page
http://www.clas.ufl.edu/users/gthursby/taoism/

This is a meta site for Daoism, which is fairly well represented on the web, with numerous links to texts, resources, and to other websites.

Taoist Studies on the World Wide Web
http://helios.unive.it/~pregadio/taoism.html
The Daoist Studies website contains translations of texts, bibliographies, information on scholarly associations and activities, and links to other related websites.

Daoist Studies
http://www.daoiststudies.org/
Daoist Studies is a "primarily intended for academic students of Daoism." It contains a bibliography of over 2,000 works in Western and Asian languages, abstracts of Ph.D. dissertations, a database of scholars, course syllabi, and links to related sites.

The Golden Elixir
http://helios.unive.it/~dsao//pregadio/index.html
Created by Fabrizio Pregadio, this site provides an introduction to Chinese alchemy. It includes articles, essays, texts in translation and in Chinese, a bibliography, and links to related topics.

Shamanism
http://www.let.leidenuniv.nl/bth/shamanism.htm
This site contains a bibliography of shamanism prepared by Barend ter Haar.

Falun Gong
http://www.let.leidenuniv.nl/bth/falun.htm
Another creation of Barend ter Haar, this site presents "an introductory analysis of the Falun Gong movement in Chinese society and culture from the perspective of the scholar of traditional Chinese religious culture." It also contains an extensive bibliography.

China: Falun Gong (or Falun Dafa)
http://www.louisville.edu/library/ekstrom/govpubs/international/china/falungong.html
This site contains links to BBC reports on Falun Gong, a U.S. government policy statement, and the Falun Gong website.

Public Health

World Resources Institute
http://www.wri.org/wri/wri/wr-98-99/prc-ntro.htm

The World Resource Institute describes itself as an "environmental think tank." This link will take you to a downloadable report on China's health and environment.

Joint U.N. Program on HIV/AIDS in China
http://www.unchina.org/unaids/eus.html

This United Nations site includes documents, essays, and contact information regarding the problem of HIV/AIDS in China.

ECONOMY

Meta Site

Hong Kong Trade and Development Council
www.tdctrade.com

This site is a good source of up-to-date information about economic performance and policy in China. It also has links to thousands of other economic and business-related sites, many of which are in English.

Economic News

Current Economic News
http://www.taiwansecurity.org/TSR-ECOSO.htm

This link from the *Taiwan Security Research* website (see **Politics** above) keeps abreast of economic news drawing on major English-language new outlets including The New York Times, CNN, The Economist, and others.

China Economic Review
http://www.chinaeconomicreview.com/

This site is an index to articles that appear in the China Economic Review. The topics covered range from acquisitions and mergers to unemployment. Unfortunately, access to full text requires a subscription.

Ministry of Foreign Trade and Economic Cooperation (MOFTEC)
http://www.moftec.gov.cn/moftec_en/index.html

The official site of MOFTEC provides relatively abundant English-language information on the economy and economic policy.

China: Economy, Industry, Business and Labor
http://www.louisville.edu/library/ekstrom/govpubs/international/china/chinaecon.html

This site contains links to economic information supplied by U.S. and Chinese government sources. It also has links to other types of information from Chinese and American government sources.

Economic Development

World Bank East Asia: Social Policy and Governance
http://www.worldbank.org/eapsocial/

This link on the World Bank website archives web links, downloadable reports and statistics broadly related to economic development. The site includes information for the entire East Asia and Pacific region.

Labor

China Labour Bulletin
http://www.china-labour.org.hk/iso/index.adp
(See **Society** above.)

CULTURE

Meta Sites

MCLC Resource Center
http://deall.ohio-state.edu/denton.2/biblio.htm

This is the ultimate Chinese culture meta site. It provides articles, bibliographies and Internet links related to literature, music, media, visual arts, education, online journals, institutions, e-texts, and translations. Affiliated with the print journal, *Modern Chinese Literature and Culture*, this site is an essential starting point for anyone with a serious scholarly interest in Internet resources on all aspects of Chinese culture.

China the Beautiful
http://www.chinapage.com/china-rm.html

This cultural site has links to everything from Beijing opera, to martial arts. It is strong on literature but also includes popular culture.

Art

Chinese-art.com
http://www.chinese-art.com/index_nonflash.htm

This "portal to the world of Chinese art" has images of both traditional and contemporary Chinese art along with articles and explanations.

China: 5,000 Years
http://kaladarshan.arts.ohio-state.edu/exhib/gug/intr/intropage2.html

This site includes a wealth of images of modern Chinese art, from the late Qing to present times.

National Palace Museum
http://www.npm.gov.tw/english/index-e.htm

This website of the National Palace Museum in Taiwan includes virtual tours of the museum's extensive holdings.

Minneapolis Institute of Art
http://www.artsmia.org/arts-of-asia/china/

Several hundred art objects from Neolithic to Qing are online at this site.

Asian Art
http://www.asianart.com

Covering all of Asia, you can find information on Chinese art associations, exhibitions, articles, and galleries.

Art Scene China
http://www.artscenechina.com/asc2002/1.htm#QuickLinks

This site contains portfolios for more than twenty contemporary China artists.

Calligraphy

Calligraphy of the Masters
http://chinapage.com/callig1.html
    This site contains samples from some of the greatest Chinese calligraphers, links to related sites, and articles and essays on modern forms of calligraphy.

Chinese Calligraphy
http://zinnia.umfacad.maine.edu/~mshea/China/callig.html#Top
    Created by Marilyn Shea, this site has a comprehensive bibliography of Western language works on Chinese calligraphy.

Film and Video

MCLC Resource Center: Media
http://deall.ohio-state.edu/denton.2/filmbib.htm
    This branch of Modern *MCLC Resource Center* is a treasure trove of resources on film, television, and print culture that includes general reference works, online resources, interviews, film scripts, and bibliographies.

Asian Film Connection (USC)
http://www.usc.edu/isd/archives/asianfilm/china/
    This is an excellent site for information on current trends in the Chinese film industry. It also includes sample course syllabi and useful links to film-related websites.

Chinese Movie Database
http://www.dianying.com/en/
    In addition to the database of Chinese films, this site includes a movie poster gallery, film-related links, a bibliography of works on film, and a discussion forum.

Media Resources Center, Moffitt Library UC Berkeley
http://www.lib.berkeley.edu/MRC/CJKVid.html#china

This site includes the extensive film and video holdings of the Moffitt Library at UC Berkeley. Each item is annotated and some entries include links to reviews.

A Chinese Cinema Page
http://www.chinesecinemas.org/index.html

Designed by Shelly Kraicer, this site is useful for locating reviews of recent Chinese films.

Facets Multi-Media
http://www.facets.org/

Facets Multi-Media is a nonprofit media arts organization which has one nation's largest video libraries for renting and buying world cinema, independent film and fine arts programming. Their online annotated catalog includes a large selection of Chinese film and documentary video.

Asian Educational Media
http://www.aems.uiuc.edu/index.las

(See **Curriculum and Teaching** above.)

Posters

Stefan Landsberger's Chinese Propaganda Poster Pages
http://www.iisg.nl/~landsberger/

This site contains more than 1,300 propaganda posters that span earliest mass movements of the 1950s to the recent crackdown on Falun Gong. Stefan Landsberger also categorizes and annotates each poster, providing context for the wealth of images presented on this excellent site.

China Posters Online
http://www.wmin.ac.uk/china/cataloguelist.htm

This site has over five hundred posters that span the period from the Cultural Revolution to the 1980s

Language and Linguistics

China Links
http://www.deall.ohio-state.edu/chan.9/c-links.htm
    Created by Marjorie Chan, this site has annotated links to over six hundred China-, Chinese language-, and linguistics-related websites.

Popular Culture and Performances

Folk Performances
http://deall.ohio-state.edu/bender.4/perform/default.htm
    This page provides links to sites on Beijing opera, puppetry, festivals and other forms of folk and performance art.

The China Experience: China Culture Index
http://www.chinavista.com/experience/index.html
    Folk arts, handicrafts, and popular culture are well represented on this site.

Chinese Furniture
http://www.chinese-furniture.com/c_resources/books.html
    This site contains an extensive bibliography of works on Chinese furniture.

Martial Arts
http://www.uvm.edu/~chinese/chingf.htm
    This site supplies links to websites related to Chinese martial arts including *taiji quan* and Shaolin *gongfu*.

Chinese Festivals
http://chinasite.com/Culture/Festival.html

Video and Film

Over the past two decades there has been no shortage of excellent documentary and feature films about China. As in the case of web resources, it is impossible to keep pace with all the latest video and film on China. The purpose of this section is to provide some suggestions that will be useful for teaching an introductory level course on contemporary China. Each section of the study guide includes recommendations of documentary video and feature films, but these represent only a small sample of the available resources. As noted in the online resources section (see above, **Culture, Film and Video**), there are a number of very useful websites related to Chinese documentary and feature cinema. For teaching purposes, a handy starting point is the Asian Educational Media website (http://www.aems.uiuc.edu/index.las). This site has a database that can be searched using four criteria: region/country, subject, media type, and audience. Searching on East Asia/China will yield over a thousand entries but this is misleading. Some items are listed multiple times or under slightly different names. Nevertheless, the database contains hundreds of annotated entries, ordering information, and some reviews.

Multi-part Series

Since the opening of China in the early 1980s, foreign documentary makers have produced several multi-part series. One of the earliest and most comprehensive series was *The Chinese*, which is based on the awarding-winning documentary, *The Heart of the Dragon*. The series is divided into twenty-six hour-long segments making it convenient for classroom use. The topics include history, social control, ideology, health care, foreign trade, culture, and technology. Filmed in the early 1980s, the only problem with this series is that China has changed tremendously since early days of the post-Mao era. After two decades of steady economic growth, twenty-first-century China bears only slight resemblance to that of the country in transition in the early 1980s. Still the series offers some fascinating, if now outdated, vignettes of life in China and, thanks to the generosity of the John D. and Catherine T. MacArthur Foundation, over 2,000 public libraries have copies of this series available for loan.

Several additional documentary series have been produced in the 1990s. *The Celestial Empire—Path of the Dragon* explores the economic and social changes of the post-Mao era in historical perspective in a series of twenty-six-minute videos. The original series was in thirteen parts and five additional segments have been added. The BBC's *The Giant Awakes* is a three-part series divided into fifty-minute segments that examine the development of capitalism, human rights, and the privatization of industry. *China: Unleashing the Dragon* is a four-part series that examines the Deng Xiaoping's role in launching reforms, and the economic, social, and cultural impact of reform. Finally, the Long Bow Group's series, *All Under Heaven: Life in a Chinese Village*, consists of several intimate looks at one north China village. The film was shot in 1986 but its intimate examination of a single village is timeless. Also of note from the Long Bow Group is *The Gate of Heavenly Peace*, a documentary on the Tiananmen crisis. In addition to the titles suggested in each unit of the study guide, information on other documentaries on a wide variety of topics can be found at the *Asian Educational Media* website: http://www.aems.uiuc.edu/index.las.

Feature Films

Chinese cinema has enjoyed widespread international recognition over the past two decades. Mainland Chinese filmmakers such as Chen Kaige, Zhang Yimou, Xie Fei, and Tian Zhuangzhuang, to name a few of the better known artists, have earned the praise and respect of critics everywhere. Chinese feature films provide invaluable teaching resources. It should be noted that however that several of the best films have running times of over two hours, making it difficult to screen them during normal class times. Specific suggestions for Chinese feature films are included in each unit of the study guide above but new films are released every year. See the *MCLC Resource Center* (http://deall.ohio-state.edu/denton.2/filmbib.htm), *Chinese Movie Database* (www.dianying.com/en/), and *Asian Film Connection* (USC) (www.usc.edu/isd/archives/asianfilm/china/), all useful sites for locating information on the burgeoning Chinese film industry.

Suggested Documentary and Feature Films

Geography and History

Documentary Video: *The Chinese: Eating; China in Revolution; China: The Mao Years.*

Feature Film: *The Emperor and the Assassin; The Opium War; Ju Dou*

Politics

Documentary Video: *China: The Mao Years, Gate of Heavenly Peace.*

Feature Film: *The Blue Kite, To Live*

Society

Documentary Video: *The Chinese: Marrying, In Search of China*

Feature Film: *The Story of Qiu Ju, Not One Less*

Economy

Documentary Video: *The Chinese: Living, The Chinese: Working, The Chinese: Trading*

Feature Film: *Happy Times, Shower*

Culture

Documentary Video: *The Chinese: Creating, The Peony Pavilion*

Feature Film: *Farewell My Concubine*

Appendix: Pronunciation Guide

The pinyin system of romanization, adopted in the People's Republic of China after 1949, has increasingly replaced the older Wade-Giles system in contemporary Western writings on China. Students will encounter both forms in *CHINA*. The simple guidelines below will help students pronounce Chinese words spelled in pinyin; the more extensive chart that follows will help them recognize alternative spellings of the names of persons, places and things.

Pinyin Pronunciation Guide

Pinyin letters have approximately the same sounds as in English, with the following exceptions:

Consonants

c: sounds like *ts* in **its**
q: sounds like *ch* in **China**
x: sounds like *sh* in **shell**
zh: sounds like *j* in **jump**

Vowels

e: sounds like the *e* in **talent**
e: when directly before ng, sounds like *u* in **lung**
o: sounds like *aw* in **saw**
ou: sounds like o in **go**

Pinyin/Wade-Giles Conversion

Pinyin	Wade-Giles	Pinyin	Wade-Giles
a	a	chan	ch'an
ai	ai	chang	ch'ang
an	an	chao	ch'ao
ang	ang	che	ch'e
ao	ao	chen	ch'en
ba	pa	cheng	ch'eng
bai	pai	chi	ch'ih
ban	pan	chong	ch'ung
bang	pang	chou	ch'ou
bao	pao	chu	ch'u
bei	pei	chuai	ch'uai
ben	pen	chuan	ch'uan
bi	pi	chuang	ch'uang
bian	pian	chui	ch'ui
biao	piao	chun	ch'un
bie	pieh	chuo	ch'o
bin	pin	ci	tz'u
bing	ping	cong	ts'ung
bo	po	cou	ts'ou
bou	pou	cu	ts'u
bu	pu	cuan	ts'uan
ca	ts'a	cui	ts'ui
cai	ts'ai	cun	ts'un
can	ts'an	cuo	ts'uo
cang	ts'ang	da	ta
cao	ts'ao	dai	tai
ce	ts'e	dan	tan
cen	ts'en	dang	tang
ceng	ts'eng	dao	tao
cha	ch'a	de	te
chai	ch'ai	dei	tei
diao	tiao	di	ti

Pinyin	Wade-Giles	Pinyin	Wade-Giles
die	tieh	dian	tien
ding	ting	gu	ku
diu	tiu	gua	kua
dong	tung	guai	kuai
dou	tou	guan	kuan
du	tu	guang	kuang
duan	tuan	gui	kuei
dui	tui	gun	kun
dun	tun	guo	kuo
duo	to	hai	hai
e	e,o	han	han
ei	ei	hang	hang
en	en	hao	hao
eng	eng	he	he, ho
er	erh	hei	hei
fa	fa	hen	hen
fan	fan	heng	heng
fang	fang	hong	hung
fei	fei	hou	hou
fen	fen	hu	hu
feng	feng	hua	hua
fo	fo	huai	huai
fou	fou	huan	huan
fu	fu	huang	huang
ga	ka	hui	hui
gai	kai	hun	hun
gan	kan	huo	huo
gao	kao	ji	chi
ge	ke, ko	jia	chia
gei	kei	jian	chien
gen	ken	jiang	chiang
geng	keng	jiao	chiao
gong	kung	jie	chieh
gou	kou	jin	chin

Pinyin	Wade-Giles	Pinyin	Wade-Giles
jiong	chiung	jing	ching
jiu	chiu	liao	liao
ju	chü	lie	lieh
juan	chüan	lin	lin
jue	chüeh	ling	ling
jun	chün	liu	liu
ka	k'a	long	lung
kai	k'ai	lou	lou
kan	k'an	lu	lu
kao	k'ao	luan	luan
ke	k'e, k'o	lun	lun
ken	k'en	luo	lo
keng	k'eng	lü	lü
kong	k'ung	lüe	lüeh
kou	k'ou	ma	ma
ku	k'u	mai	mai
kua	k'ua	man	man
kuai	k'uai	mang	mang
kuan	k'uan	mao	mao
kuang	k'uang	mei	mei
kui	k'uei	men	men
kun	k'un	meng	meng
kuo	k'uo	mi	mi
la	la	mian	mien
lai	lai	miao	miao
lan	lan	mie	mieh
lang	lang	min	min
lao	lao	ming	ming
le	le	miu	miu
lei	lei	mo	mo
leng	leng	mou	mou
li	li	mu	mu
lia	lia	na	na
lian	lien	nai	nai

Pinyin	Wade-Giles	Pinyin	Wade-Giles
liang	liang	nan	nan
nao	nao	nang	nang
ne	ne	ping	p'ing
nei	nei	pu	`p'u
nen	nen	qi	ch'i
neng	neng	qia	ch'ia
ni	ni	qian	ch'ien
nian	nien	qiang	ch'iang
niang	niang	qiao	ch'iao
niao	niao	qie	ch'ieh
nie	nieh	qin	ch'in
nin	nin	qing	ch'ing
ning	ning	qiong	ch'iung
niu	niu	qiu	ch'iu
nong	nung	qu	ch'ü
nou	nou	quan	ch'üan
nu	nu	que	ch'üeh
nuan	nuan	qun	ch'ün
nuo	no	ran	jan
nü	nü	rang	jang
nue	nüeh	rao	jao
pa	p'a	re	je
pai	p'ai	ren	jen
pan	p'an	reng	jeng
pang	p'ang	ri	jih
pao	p'ao	rong	jong
pei	p'ei	rou	jou
pen	p'en	ru	ju
peng	p'eng	ruan	juan
po	p'o	rui	jui
pou	p'ou	run	jun
pi	p'i	ruo	jo
pian	p'ien	sa	sa
piao	p'iao	sai	sai

Pinyin	Wade-Giles	Pinyin	Wade-Giles
pie	p'ieh	san	san
pin	p'in	sang	sang
se	se	sao	sao
sen	sen	te	t'e
seng	seng	teng	t'eng
sha	sha	ti	t'i
shai	shai	tian	t'ien
shan	shan	tiao	t'iao
shang	shang	tie	t'ieh
shao	shao	ting	t'ing
she	she	tong	t'ung
shei	shei	tou	t'ou
shen	shen	tu	t'u
sheng	sheng	tuan	t'uan
shi	shih	tui	t'ui
shou	shou	tun	t'un
shu	shu	tuo	t'o
shua	shua	wa	wa
shuai	shuai	wai	wai
shuan	shuan	wan	wan
shuang	shuang	wang	wang
shui	shui	wei	wei
shun	shun	wen	wen
shuo	shuo	weng	weng
si	szu	wo	wo
song	sung	wu	wu
sou	sou	xi	hsi
su	su	xia	hsia
suan	suan	xian	hsien
sui	sui	xiag	hsiang
sun	sun	xiao	hsiao
suo	so	xie	hsieh
ta	t'a	xin	hsin
tai	t'ai	xing	hsing

Pinyin	Wade-Giles	Pinyin	Wade-Giles
tan	t'an	xiong	hsiung
tang	t'ang	xiu	hsiu
tao	t'ao	xu	hsü
xue	hsüeh	xuan	hsüan
xun	hsün	zhan	chan
ya	ya	zhang	chang
yan	yen	zhao	chao
yang	yang	zhe	che
yao	yao	zhei	chei
ye	yeh	zhen	chen
yi	i	zheng	cheng
yin	yin	zhi	chih
ying	ying	zhong	chung
yong	yung	zhou	chou
you	yu	zhu	chu
yu	yü	zhua	chua
yuan	yüan	zhuai	chuai
yue	yüeh	zhuan	chuan
yun	yün	zhuang	chuang
za	tsa	zhui	chui
zai	tsai	zhun	chun
zan	tsan	zhuo	cho
zang	tsang	zi	tzu
zao	tsao	zong	tsung
ze	tse	zou	tsou
zei	tsei	zu	tsu
zen	tsen	zuan	tsuan
zeng	tseng	zui	tsui
zha	cha	zun	tun
zhai	chai	zuo	tso